T0329169

Cambridge Elements ≡

Elements in Reinventing Capitalism
edited by
Arie Y. Lewin
Duke University
Till Talaulicar
University of Erfurt

THE NEW ENLIGHTENMENT

Reshaping Capitalism and the Global Order in the 21st Century

Edited by

Arie Y. Lewin
Duke University

Greg Linden
University of California, Berkeley

David J. Teece
University of California, Berkeley

CAMBRIDGE
UNIVERSITY PRESS

University Printing House, Cambridge CB2 8BS, United Kingdom

One Liberty Plaza, 20th Floor, New York, NY 10006, USA

477 Williamstown Road, Port Melbourne, VIC 3207, Australia

314–321, 3rd Floor, Plot 3, Splendor Forum, Jasola District Centre,
New Delhi – 110025, India

103 Penang Road, #05–06/07, Visioncrest Commercial, Singapore 238467

Cambridge University Press is part of the University of Cambridge.

It furthers the University's mission by disseminating knowledge in the pursuit of
education, learning, and research at the highest international levels of excellence.

www.cambridge.org
Information on this title: www.cambridge.org/9781009258630
DOI: 10.1017/9781009258616

© Cambridge University Press & Assessment 2022

First published 2022

A catalogue record for this publication is available from the British Library.

ISBN 978-1-009-25863-0 Paperback
ISSN 2634-8950 (online)
ISSN 2634-8942 (print)

The New Enlightenment

Reshaping Capitalism and the Global Order in the 21st Century

Elements in Reinventing Capitalism

DOI: 10.1017/9781009258616
First published online: August 2022

Arie Y. Lewin
Duke University

Greg Linden
University of California, Berkeley

David J. Teece
University of California, Berkeley

Editor for correspondence: Arie Y. Lewin, ayl3@duke.edu

Abstract: The *Reinventing Capitalism* series seeks to feature explorations of the crisis of legitimacy facing capitalism today, including the increasing income and wealth gap, the decline of the middle class, threats to employment due to globalization and digitalization, undermined trust in institutions, discrimination against minorities, global poverty, and pollution. The series is a collection of authoritative literature reviews of foundational topics on renewing capitalism. Being grounded in a business and management perspective, the series incorporates insights from multiple disciplines that promise to substantiate the causes of the current crisis and potential solutions regarding what needs to be done. This Element provides an overview of the series and explains the background of its development; it contains eight sections that deal with various facets of the subject from the perspectives of a group of top-notch authors.

Keywords: corporate governance, deglobalization, future of work, inequality, management ideologies

ISBNs: 9781009258630 (PB), 9781009258616 (OC)
ISSNs: 2634-8950 (online), 2634-8942 (print)

Contents

Contributors

- **Gerald F. Davis**
  University of Michigan
- **Maryann Feldman**
  University of North Carolina–Chapel Hill
- **Frederick Guy**
  University of London
- **Simona Iammarino**
  London School of Economics and Political Science
- **Carolin Ioramashvili**
  London School of Economics and Political Science
- **William Lazonick**
  University of Massachusetts–Lowell
- **Arie Y. Lewin**
  Duke University
- **Greg Linden**
  University of California–Berkeley
- **Ted Ryan**
  Duke University
- **Orville Schell**
  Center on U.S.–China Relations at the Asia Society
- **Craig Smith**
  University of Glasgow
- **Till Talaulicar**
  University of Erfurt
- **David J. Teece**
  University of California–Berkeley
- **Sarah Koehane Williamson**
  FCLTGlobal

1 Introduction: The New Enlightenment

Arie Y. Lewin, Greg Linden, and David J. Teece

In July 2019, an international array of leading policymakers, academics, and business leaders came together for *the New Enlightenment*, a conference devoted to understanding the opportunities for reshaping capitalism. The conference took place in Edinburgh at Panmure House, where Adam Smith lived and worked over two centuries ago.[1] Speakers included former UK prime minister Gordon Brown, the historian Niall Ferguson, the economist John Kay, and Weijian Shan, head of the Hong Kong–based private equity firm PAG Group.[2]

The conference was conceived by one of us (Teece), who was in turn stimulated by exchanges with his friend and Edinburgh Business School (EBS) colleague, Neil Kay. Kay was, at the time, helping to provide a vision for the renovated historic home of Adam Smith that former academic director Keith Lumsden had purchased on behalf of the EBS. Teece and like-minded colleagues had serious forebodings about the stresses disrupting Western economies, about the way China has begun to reposition itself technologically and militarily, and about the mounting opprobrium directed toward large corporations. An awareness has emerged that the liberal democracies and the rule of law–governed global economy – which had seemed quite robust just thirty years earlier with the collapse of the Soviet Union – were facing a deep and still evolving existential challenge. It was clear that wide-ranging conversations needed to take place to delve into and explore the antecedents and implications of the growing disenchantment with globalization and the conduct of large banks and corporations. The simultaneous intersections of multiple, massive global challenges seemed to require new models and novel mindsets.

In Edinburgh, over the course of three days, the effort to explore the interconnected issues holistically and work toward potential solutions got underway in plenary and breakout sessions and at two memorable dinners. The general focus was on two tracks: what companies can and should do to better align their interests with those of their stakeholders; and how major external events are likely to reshape the business environment. In particular, the informal

---

[1] Academic cosponsors included Edinburgh's Heriot-Watt University, the Edinburgh Business School, the Haas Business School of University of California – Berkeley, and the David Eccles School of Business of the University of Utah. Corporate cosponsors included German insurer FWU AG, American Discovery Capital, and the Berkeley Research Group. The conference would not have been possible without the generous support of all the sponsors.

[2] Full details of the conference are available at www.panmure2019.com, including links to videos of the sessions.

discussions during breaks, meals, and walks between locations surfaced an array of issues including the undercurrents driving short-termism, the need to better incentivize long-term investing and innovation, the insularity of corporate governance, the undesirable side effects of shareholder value maximization, the challenge of the unfolding digital industrial revolution, the changing nature of work, the emergence of new powerful tech giants, and the forces driving deglobalization and the gradual decoupling of the world's two largest economies.

Underlying the discussions was a collective aspiration to revisit and renew Adam Smith's holistic perspective, not just as an economist but as a moral philosopher, by openly engaging why capitalism, which has generated so much wealth and progress, is increasingly deemed to be failing so many. The sources of concern are everywhere: the depth and breadth of unequal opportunities, social injustice, widening of income and wealth gaps, disparities in life expectancy, housing shortages, uneven access to medical care, perceived inequality in primary and secondary education, and the disjuncture between education and the labor market.

Clearly, the range of potential topics is vast, hence the opportunity for this new Cambridge University Press Element Series on Reinventing Capitalism, the brainchild of Professor Arie Lewin of Duke University and coedited with Professor Till Talaulicar of Germany's University of Erfurt. How firms operate and how they are perceived are profoundly affected by the major global problems of the age: systemic and growing inequality, the fragmentation of the global datasphere, the rise of illiberalism, and the existential challenge of global warming. By the same token, firms can opt to be part of the solution, and some are beginning to undertake their own initiatives (e.g., Mars' Economics of Mutuality, see Badger 2020).

In his 2021 annual letter to CEOs, Larry Fink, the founder and CEO of the BlackRock investment fund, observed that the COVID-19 pandemic revealed and highlighted challenges associated with deeper trends, including a growing retirement crisis, systemic inequalities, historic protests for racial justice, and deep political alienation powered by social networks and political opportunism (Fink 2021). But the letter also takes note of companies that were motivated to focus on their stakeholders and innovate to keep food and goods flowing during lockdowns and that have stepped up to support nonprofits serving those in need. The same letter concludes by noting that, amid all the disruption in 2020, many corporations adopted policies and strategies to address climate risk.

Clearly, there is some evidence that companies can play a positive role in the quest for solutions to the many national and global challenges in which they are directly or indirectly implicated. Corporate leaders, separately and through industry-spanning organizations such as Inclusive Capitalism (under the leadership of Lady Lynn Forester de Rothschild), have the opportunity to engage their workforces with a broader purpose that encompasses the search for solutions to big problems of unequal opportunities writ large, and also to advance national discourse directly and through advocacy with policymakers. Today's complex challenges demand the active participation and cooperation of every sector of society.

Before concluding the Edinburgh conference, a majority of attendees voted in support of a Panmure declaration that called on government leaders to recommit to ethically based democracy and to protect the freedom and well-being of the communities in their care.[3] But it was clear that this was a beginning, not a conclusion.

On July 31, 2020, during the COVID-19 pandemic restrictions, there was a follow-up online event called "One Year On" that updated the major conference themes: the need to reform corporate governance and the changing structure of globalization. There was much to update and process, including the Business Roundtable's support for stakeholder capitalism (Business Roundtable 2019), the increasing assertiveness of China, and the disruption of global trade due to the pandemic, which accelerated the trend toward deglobalization and decoupling of sources of production and global supply chains.

The present Element, which includes contributions from several of the speakers at the Edinburgh conference as well as other distinguished academics, seeks to extend and expand the conversation still further. Our goal in this volume – and in the new Cambridge Elements series that it inaugurates – is to advance the work that began in the home of Adam Smith by juxtaposing multiple perspectives so as to generate new insights into the nature of purposeful stakeholder capitalism.

The Reinventing Capitalism series will feature explorations of various aspects of the crisis of legitimacy facing capitalism today. The series is intended to be a collection of authoritative literature reviews of foundational topics on the revitalization of the capitalist system. Contributions to the series aim to be forward-looking as well as descriptive of recent developments. While grounded in a business and management perspective, the series incorporates insights from multiple disciplines that provide insights into the causes

---

[3] "This First Declaration of Panmure House urges international leaders to base their policies and decision-making on a set of common principles, as espoused and formulated by Adam Smith, which cherish the required values of an ethically-based liberal democratic system, a moral commitment to the well-being of our communities and affirm responsibility to protect economic, political and social freedoms, use resources wisely, avoid unintentional consequences, follow the rule of law, favour markets and prices as guides to resource allocation and take a long term view of private and public investments, to support inclusive economic growth and prosperity for all."

of the current crisis and potential solutions. Subjects cover the history and development of various forms of capitalism; the relationship between capitalism, socialism, and democracy; the role of "moral sentiments" in the modern economy; capitalism and the future of corporate governance; globalization in a disaggregating world; and entrepreneurship and innovation in the modern economy.

This Element consists of eight sections in addition to this Introduction:

1. Craig Smith (University of Glasgow): Capitalism and the Legacy of Adam Smith
2. Ted Ryan (Duke University): The Failure of Shareholder Value Ideology and the Contours of a Humane Capitalism
3. William Lazonick (University of Massachusetts–Lowell): Innovation and Financialization in the Corporate Economy
4. Arie Y. Lewin (Duke University) and Till Talaulicar (University of Erfurt): Corporate Governance, CEO Compensation, and the Income Gap
5. Sarah Koehane Williamson (FCLTGlobal): Reviving Productive Capitalism: How CEOs and Boards Can Drive Sustained Value Creation
6. Gerald F. Davis (University of Michigan): Market Power and the New Antitrust: Where the Antimonopoly Narrative Goes Wrong
7. Maryann Feldman (University of North Carolina–Chapel Hill), Frederick Guy (University of London), Simona Iammarino (London School of Economics and Political Science), and Carolin Ioramashvili (London School of Economics and Political Science): The Emerging Technological Revolutions and Social Change
8. Orville Schell (Center on U.S.–China Relations at the Asia Society): How and Why Globalization Is Disaggregating: The Impact of China

Each author presents a short, insightful essay about specific problems faced by capitalism and liberal democracies as well as potential paths forward. It will be clear to even the casual reader that the authors are not always in agreement. This Element, like the series as a whole, aims to provide a sampling of some of the diverse perspectives that must be reconciled to find workable solutions; these will be developed in subsequent Elements.

Craig Smith's section on Adam Smith provides a link to the original Enlightenment. Smith's *Wealth of Nations* (1976a [1776]) has been widely lauded as the philosophical foundation of modern capitalism. For Smith, however, the workings of the economy were just one aspect of his field of endeavor, known as moral philosophy. Before the *Wealth*, he wrote *The Theory of Moral Sentiments* (1976b [1759]). In it, Smith posited that economic agents operate under shared moral constraints of right and wrong because they are part of society. He also saw a role for government in promoting desirable behavior in the marketplace.

Craig Smith argues that if Adam Smith were able to observe the economy of the twenty-first century, he would be impressed with the high standard of living but dismayed by the obsession with wealth as the basis of social status. He would recognize the balancing act required by society to enable companies to create value while restraining their anticompetitive tendencies. Rediscovering all of Adam Smith's thinking would help modern corporations, steeped in the logic of neoclassical economics, to develop new models for balancing their mission of wealth creation with the maintenance of a just society.

We shift the focus more squarely to the heart of contemporary capitalism with Ted Ryan's section, "The Failure of Shareholder Value Ideology." The dogma that the sole purpose of a firm is to make money for its shareholders is typically traced to a 1970 essay by Milton Friedman in the *New York Times*. Ryan forcefully develops the argument that maximizing shareholder value (MSV) can be self-defeating, emphasizing short-term payouts over long-term investments, and generates negative social externalities, including environmental degradation.

Ryan notes that many firms have already begun to move away from strict MSV, and he proposes grouping these efforts under the term "Purposeful All-Stakeholder" (PAS) capitalism. This builds on the idea that employees and managers will be more motivated if they see their work as serving a larger purpose for society as well as the profits of shareholders. The section concludes by pointing to companies that have already moved toward the new PAS model, including Costco, Electrolux, and Best Buy.

William Lazonick's section on "Innovation and Financialization" provides insight into one of the mechanisms favored by shareholder value maximizers, namely, the diversion of funds from long-term reinvestment in new and better products and services to short-term payouts to shareholders through dividends and share buybacks. He calls this shift the "financialization" of the firm and draws a direct line from this process to the worsening of employment opportunities, growing income inequality, and weak productivity growth. He concludes by calling for regulatory and governance reforms.

The section by Arie Lewin and Till Talaulicar on "Corporate Governance, CEO Compensation, and the Income Gap" looks at the inner workings of firms to explore why CEO compensation has grown consistently faster than the stock market for over forty years. There are numerous forces pushing in this direction. One is that the board of directors that sets the compensation package is populated in part by other CEOs who seem to favor more generous pay packages. Another problem is that the typical budgeting process allows executives to underpromise and overdeliver, setting the bar low for contingent bonuses. Executives are able to keep investors happy by shortchanging long-term strategy to meet and smooth quarterly earnings per share targets. Executives also have incentives to build "empires" through mergers and acquisitions because they can expect to be more highly compensated as the head of larger firms.

The generosity of CEO compensation interacts with the stock buybacks discussed by Lazonick. Boards of directors increasingly relied on compensating CEOs in the form of stock and options on the theory that this would better align the CEO's interests with those of shareholders. But managers are also effectively incentivized to conduct stock buybacks to raise the value of the shares they hold. Lewin and Talaulicar discuss several ways that board composition and CEO compensation plans could be designed to redirect efforts in support of the the the needs of employees and other stakeholders, rather than just shareholders.

Sarah Keohane Williamson's section on "Sustained Value Creation" addresses the complementary issue of short-termism. Evidence suggests that long-term thinking is consistent with better corporate results, yet surveys show that short-term thinking is becoming more prevalent. Williamson calls for executives and directors to embrace a long-term, stakeholder perspective, to pursue riskier strategies (appropriately analyzed) that offer the possibility of opening new lines of business, and to adjust capital allocation more frequently so as to favor promising initiatives, instead of throwing good money after bad. Companies that only follow their current business model indefinitely will ultimately disappoint their stakeholders by failing to thrive in the future.

Jerry Davis' section "Market Power and the New Antitrust" turns our attention back to how firms behave, particularly how large technology-based firms exert power over individuals and regulators, as well as how their relentless drive to increase profits often stretches the rules. Davis calls into question the conventional wisdom that we are coming to an antitrust "moment," because industries are more concentrated and consumers are being harmed, by noting that the evidence is unclear or even points in the opposite direction. Antitrust is indeed a blunt instrument to address the subtle but damaging impacts of "big tech." His main recommendation is to have a new, tech-savvy agency regulate the ability of the big platform owners (Amazon, Facebook, etc.) to control the capacity of potential rivals to grow or even get started.

Davis argues for the need to devise a new regulatory framework that sets guidelines and strict enforcing mechanisms and appropriate fines, as the European Union (EU) has done with the establishment of the General Data Protection Regulation (GDPR) – a legal framework that sets guidelines for the collection and processing of personal information from individuals who live in the EU.

Maryann Feldman, Frederick Guy, Simona Iammarino, and Carolin Ioramashvili broaden this perspective in their section on "Technological Revolutions," which considers some of the ways that platforms and artificial intelligence are driving societal changes – particularly in the workplace. In some ways, they note, workers are becoming subservient to technology that monitors or even paces their work. While noting that the impact of a tech revolution can only be properly judged in retrospect, they lean toward the hypothesis that workers will lose more ground relative to employers who use new technologies to deskill or displace current jobs.

In contrast to Davis, Feldman et al. accept the mounting evidence that market power is becoming concentrated among a smaller number of large firms, not least the owners of tech platforms. They note that the ownership of these firms is also becoming more concentrated among a few large finance companies, such as BlackRock, that manage funds for investors. Even the locations where technology is developed and wealth accumulated, such as Silicon Valley, are now more concentrated than they were in the past. They call not only for more robust regulation, including antitrust enforcement, but also for new, decentralized technologies such as blockchain that can potentially democratize the economy. Noting that more job destruction is likely in the near term, they suggest that measures such as universal basic income may be necessary to make society more resilient.

We finish by widening the lens still further to look at the major geopolitical challenge of our time in Orville Schell's section on "The Impact of China." Even as liberal democracies struggle with the internal forces described in the earlier sections, a tide of authoritarianism is rising in many parts of the world that challenges and attempts to undermine democratic arrangements such as the EU. The apotheosis of this development is Xi Jinping's China, which is in the process of reimposing Maoist principles on a country that for decades appeared to be opening outward as it modernized. Instead, China is increasingly isolating its citizens from outside influences and broadcasting its preferred forms of governance outward through its "Belt and Road" initiative of investment in key infrastructure projects around the world. And, like Russia, its neighbor and fellow authoritarian state, China is beginning to project itself militarily. This state of affairs is leading to a partial decoupling of the global economy, with some manufacturing and services spanning the divide while others, especially if they involve personal data, becoming rigorously divided. The trust and openness that underlaid the historic wealth creation of late twentieth-century capitalism has been damaged, perhaps irrevocably.

The existential challenge posed by China has immeasurably raised the stakes for renewing capitalism in liberal democracies. Our authors span a range of opinion as to whether Western capitalism – riven by the effects of poor govern-ance, technological upheaval, and uncontrolled finance – is in the process of destroying itself and whether minor adjustments or major overhauls are needed to regain the (then unnamed) stakeholder capitalism that predominated when firms were smaller, more embedded in their communities, and less subject to the forces of globalization and financial engineering. It is through the rational exchange of ideas among multiple perspectives that a New Enlightenment conversation will produce fresh insights and workable solutions.

Our goal was not to be comprehensive but to stake out the complex terrain that needs to be mapped and managed. It's as wide as global challenges (how to integrate a rising China) and as narrow as what goes on inside individual firms (reforming CEO pay and corporate boards, integrating new technologies). It's about how firms interact with investors (stock buybacks) and with each other (increased concentration among big firms). And it's also about the philosophy behind these efforts (questioning shareholder primacy, rediscovering the moral philosophy of Adam Smith). This is the territory we'll be exploring in this new Cambridge Elements series.

2 Capitalism and the Legacy of Adam Smith
Craig Smith

Adam Smith is known to the public as the founding father of capitalism, as the man who invented economics, the defender of self-interest, and apostle of free markets. These observations, like so many other widely held popular beliefs, are only partly true. If we are to look at Adam Smith's legacy in a volume devoted to reinventing capitalism, then we ought to start by noting that Smith was not an economist, but a moral philosopher who worked on a subject he understood as political economy.

Smith's contribution to the study of the economy is to be found in the clarity of his development of the basic concepts of economic analysis. How we understand the economy today has largely been shaped by the *Wealth of Nations* (Smith 1976a [1776]), but that book was part of a wider system of thought that Smith developed throughout his life and it is complemented by his great work of moral philosophy, *The Theory of Moral Sentiments* (Smith 1976b [1759]). Smith's views on political economy exist within a moral framework, and the same agents who compete in the marketplace cooperate and associate in other social settings. Our beliefs about how we ought to behave in our economic life are constrained by our moral beliefs about right and wrong.

Smith could not be clearer about this. Indeed, he starts the *Moral Sentiments* by denying that human beings are dominated by self-interest. As he puts it: "How selfish soever man may be supposed, there are evidently some principles in his nature, which interest him in the fortune of others, and render their happiness necessary to him, though he derives nothing from it except the pleasure of seeing it" (Smith 1976b [1759]: 9). Smith had no truck with crude abstractions such as *homo economicus*. The idea that humans are best understood as abstract agents, much less rational utility maximizers whose behavior can be predicted with accuracy, cuts against the spirit of Smith's project. Smith took human beings as they are and sought to explain all the complexities of their behavior.[4]

While academic specialization has caused the discipline of economics to become separated from those of moral philosophy and political science, it is important to note that this was not the case for Smith. His subject was political economy, a discipline that saw politics and economics as intimately related and which Smith taught as part of his moral philosophy lectures. What this means is

---

[4] Indeed, the best of the latest scholarship on Adam Smith focuses on *The Theory of Moral Sentiments* and Smith's writing on jurisprudence (Smith 1980b) and philosophy of science (Smith 1980a).

that it is not enough to try to understand the operation of the economic life of a nation in a manner detached from its political life or its moral beliefs. Political actors respond to economic incentives and economic actors are aware that political institutions have a profound impact on the conditions in which economic activity takes place. Both political actors and economic actors are raised in a society that has shared moral beliefs about right and wrong conduct. Smith knew this and understood that moral and political constraints would be placed on what we could expect from economic policy.

Also, on any proper reading, Smith is not a capitalist. The term "capitalism," meaning a system under which labor is alienated from ownership of the means of production, was actually popularized in the mid-nineteenth century – long after Smith had died – by early critics such as Proudhon and Marx. As with most terms invented by people who are hostile to what they are naming, it is of limited use in understanding any lessons that Smith might have to teach us. Smith did not talk of capitalism but of commercial society, a form of society which was new and very different from the types of society that had gone before it. Commercial societies, Smith saw, were based on exchange. They were also wealthy societies, and wealth was a good thing because it reduced poverty and, more particularly for Smith, it reduced infant mortality. This may seem crude to us today, but for Smith it was a simple and effective measure of what he called improvement. If, in a commercial society, you did not need to watch your children die from want, then your life was qualitatively better than those in earlier societies.

This argument is complemented by his analysis in the *Moral Sentiments*. There, Smith argued that human beings are moral creatures possessed of a deep capacity to sympathize with one another. He noted that poverty and suffering limited our opportunities to sympathize with others. If we are desperately trying to stay alive, then our attention is focused on our own needs. If our lives are characterized by suffering and misery, then we learn to suppress our emotions and concern for others as a survival mechanism (Smith 1976b [1759]: 205). But once subsistence becomes secure we are able to give greater play to our emotions and devote time to expressing our concern for others. Smith believed that "A humane and polished people, who have more sensibility to the passions of others, can more readily enter into an animated and passionate behaviour" (Smith 1976b [1759]: 207). He talks about the natural circles of sympathy where we feel most for those closest to us, our emotional connection becoming more shallow as the people concerned become more distant from us. He realized that this was a natural feature of human behavior, but he also realized that growing wealth and security allowed those circles to widen and our sympathy to deepen.

Smith's recognition that we can widen and deepen our sympathy the wealthier we become did not lead him to make a crude judgment that richer societies were necessarily more moral societies. Wealth brought its own moral dangers and it is here that the *Moral Sentiments* really comes into conversation with the *Wealth of Nations*. Early on in the *Moral Sentiments*, Smith discusses how our ability to sympathize with other people is a basic feature of human nature. We imagine ourselves in another person's situation and approve or disapprove of their behavior depending on how it matches our idea of what we would do were we in their shoes. Crucially, Smith combines this with the observation that humans are sociable and want to be liked by others. As a result we begin to shape our behavior so that it gains the approval of our peers. Society is a "mirror" (Smith 1976b [1759]: 110) in which we see ourselves reflected back in the reactions of others. The result is the creation of an intricate moral psychology where Smith explains how we internalize the opinions of others and organically develop a shared set of moral beliefs.

However, Smith is aware that this desire to be admired and approved of by others has other, less savory, aspects. He is very clear that the desire to increase our wealth is to be understood as driven by our desire to secure the goods that make us the object of approval. We see the lives of the rich and famous and we want to be like them. We want a slice of that life because we think that the conveniences that they enjoy will make our lives more comfortable and, even more importantly, make other people admire us. For Smith this is the origin of rank in society, and it explains why the poor admire the rich. We follow celebrities not because we hope to gain favor from them, but because we are able to live vicariously through them. We see their gilded lives and that gives us an idea of convenience and happiness that drives us to work hard to afford the indicators of prestige that are the basis of the phenomenon of fashion. We want people to admire us and wealth is a means to draw the attention of others.

Most of our pursuit of wealth is for display, rather than material needs. The pursuit of frivolities, rather than necessities, is the engine of commercial society. Smith's point is that this creates the conditions in which the poor are able to secure both the necessities and some of the conveniences of human life while at the same time being able to enjoy freedom from absolute dependence on their social superiors. In the past we obeyed our feudal lords because if we did not we would starve. The political implication of this was that they could demand that we go to war for them. Now, they have lost the power to have such an impact on our lives. In a commercial society we sell our goods or labor to many potential customers or employers, none of whom has absolute power over us. As the holders of feudal power lose their ability to command force and disrupt the political order, so we see the rise of the rule of law and the nation-state.

Having explained how commercial society has dispensed with absolute poverty, Smith goes on to develop a notion of poverty that is focused on the meaning of status in a society. His argument is that to have social status the members of society must possess a certain level of material goods, and this level of goods differs in each society. The process of pursuing wealth to seek status is driven not so much by what you have as by what the things you have mean in interpersonal comparison.

> Though it is in order to supply the necessities and conveniences of the body, that the advantages of external fortune are originally recommended to us, we cannot live long in the world without perceiving that the respect of our equals, our credit and rank in the society we live in, depend very much upon the degree in which we possess, or are supposed to possess, those advantages. The desire of becoming the proper objects of this respect, of deserving and obtaining this credit and rank among our equals, is, perhaps, the strongest of all our desires. (Smith 1976b [1759]: 212–213)

Smith's discussion of this is a masterpiece of detached analysis. He offers us the parable of the "poor man's son" (Smith 1976b [1759]: 181) whom heaven has cursed with ambition and who spends his whole life working hard to get the gadgets and clothing of the wealthy. He works long hours and neglects his family and friends in the belief that when he secures these goods they will make him happy. But when he finally achieves success and secures the goods enjoyed by the rich, he realizes that they do not constitute real happiness. If Smith had left things there we might be tempted to see a contradiction in his thinking, an "Adam Smith Problem" as it used to be called, where the positive account of self-interest as the route to wealth in the *Wealth of Nations* is opposed by the account in the *Moral Sentiments*, where self-interested pursuit of material gain is shown to be hollow and destructive of true happiness. But Smith has something else in mind. He points out that the "deception" (Smith 1976b [1759]: 183) that leads the poor man to pursue wealth is a deception that leads to the generation of wealth that benefits others. The poor man's son works hard and serves others so that he might gain, and the unintended consequence of this is that he leaves society better than it was before, even though the thing driving him leaves him no happier.

Smith was also aware that in the past this line of thinking had been taken too far and led moralists to an unnecessary contempt for the ordinary material comforts of life. This, he believed, was a mistake. The point to note was that humans had a number of different sources of happiness and that a rounded life included all of them. Focusing on a single measure of happiness or success was a fundamental misunderstanding of what it is to be human. Smith felt that those driven purely by gain were maladjusted and that this had led to a corrupted set of moral behaviors.

Once again Smith turned to his account of how we transform our judgments of the behaviors of others into shared moral beliefs. He explained how humans learn to internalize these judgments and the imaginative process of making them. We do this to such an extent that we create an impartial spectator in our own mind, one who judges us before we act and who knows our true motives. Using this to judge ourselves, we develop the voice of conscience. This voice speaks to us when we would put our own selfish desires before the needs of others. We "see ourselves as others see us" (Smith 1976b [1759]: 112), such that we learn to "restrain our selfish, and to indulge our benevolent affections" (Smith 1976b [1759]: 25).

Now, this does not purge us of the desire to improve our situation, but what it does do is create and enforce a set of rules about what it is fair and just to do when we are in competition with others. As Smith puts it, we are free to compete in the race of life, but we must not trip up our competitors. This is crucial to understanding Smith's world view because it explains his distrust of merchants and corporations. Smith thought that such bodies were always tempted to use the power of the state to protect themselves and stifle competition. Such actors were in effect cheating in the game of economic life.

Smith argued that the interests of the large trading companies of his day, such as the British East India Company, were rarely aligned with the interests of the country as a whole. Merchants, manufacturers, and trading companies should be viewed with some skepticism by those who are interested in the wealth of the nation. Moreover, corporations and governments can have unhealthy relationships.

The idea that a country's economic strength is measured by the balance sheet of its national champion industries is a popular idea. At best it is a case of ill-judged chauvinistic nationalism; at worst it drives the idea that trade between nations is a form of competition almost akin to war. It is also an idea that Smith utterly rejects. The wealth of a nation is not to be measured by the wealth of its merchants; it is to be measured by the standard of living of all of its people.

Merchants have their own interests and claim that these are the same as the national interest, but policies that enrich merchants by subsidizing production or raising tariffs against competition benefit the merchants at the expense of the people as a whole. A monopoly, Smith says in a telling term, is a monopoly "against" the people. It is the merchant who profits as the rest of the population pay higher prices for inferior goods. Merchants are keen to wrap themselves in the flag when it suits them, but, as Smith observes: "I have never known much good done by those who affected to trade for the public good" (Smith 1976a [1776]: 456).

Understanding the economy means understanding the political interests of economic actors. So, when Smith points to the unhealthy relationship between powerful economic actors and the government and the fact that "People of the same trade seldom meet together, even for merriment and diversion, but the conversation ends in a conspiracy against the public, or in some contrivance to raise prices" (Smith 1976a [1776]: 145), he is making both economic and political arguments grounded in his moral philosophy.

Smith provides us with a historical account of the rise of the modern state and the rule of law, and he links it to the moral psychology of just behavior. The rise of modern political institutions is both conditioned by economic change and vital to that change. The rules of justice emerge alongside the mechanism for enforcing them through law and government. It is only with the development of stable political institutions and the rule of law that commerce can realize its true potential. While this is the result of a complex historical process, the impact of the results on the lives of individuals is remarkably straightforward: "when they are secure of enjoying the fruits of their industry, they naturally exert it to better their condition, and to acquire not only the necessaries, but the conveniences and elegances of life" (Smith 1976a [1776]: 405).

There may have been problems and potential corruption that resulted from this new way of living, but in many important respects it was transforming the lives of ordinary people and allowing them access to a standard of living undreamt of by their ancestors. This, according to Smith, is what constitutes wealth. It is not the amount of gold in a country's treasury, the splendor of its monarch, or the profits of its merchants. It is ordinary people's access to the necessities and conveniences of human life. What Smith wanted was to understand how this new type of society operated. How was it able to produce such improvements in productive outputs and what dangers did it face?

So, Smith was neither an economist nor a capitalist, but this does not mean that his work has no lessons for those of us trying to understand the nature of the economy in which we live. Moreover, the acuity of Smith's analysis means that his work contains key observations that can help us to reimagine how capitalism might operate. But that is only possible if we recognize that the Smith of the *Wealth of Nations* is also the Smith of the *Moral Sentiments* and *Lectures on Jurisprudence* – a very good reason for more economists to read more moral philosophy and political science as they try to understand the modern economy.

What might Smith make of twenty-first-century capitalism? He would very much recognize the balancing act in developed economies between the corporations that create wealth and the rules that are set to restrain their anticompetitive efforts. He would undoubtedly marvel at how standards of living have continued to rise, yet deplore the tendency to make conspicuous displays of wealth the basis of social status. Smith believed that true status should be based on virtuous behavior and he saw an important role for government in helping to promote virtue and culture by encouraging broader education. Adam Smith is very far from the caricatured defender of corporate greed he is sometimes taken for, and he is far less averse to government action to address collective problems than many people think. His thinking is a powerful source of inspiration to address our contemporary problems.

3 The Failure of Shareholder Value Ideology and the Contours of a Humane Capitalism

Ted Ryan

Introduction

Eventually, inevitably, false ideas die. The obituaries for the "maximizing shareholder value" (MSV) ideology continue to accumulate. Three eminent corporate governance experts, Colin Mayer, Leo Strine, and Jaap Winter, wrote a *Fortune Magazine* article titled "50 years later, Milton Friedman's shareholder doctrine is dead" (Mayer, Strine, & Winter 2020).

In 2019, the Business Roundtable, consisting of 181 CEOs of major US corporations, revised its purpose statement from maximizing shareholder value to "a fundamental commitment to all of our stakeholders. ... Each of our stakeholders is essential. We commit to deliver value to all of them, for the future success of our companies, our communities and our country" (Business Roundtable 2019).

McKinsey & Company declared that it is time to move beyond the maximizing shareholder value model. Its 2020 report states, "Business leaders should . . . make the choice to demonstrate that they see their mission as serving not only shareholders but also customers, suppliers, workers, and communities. The common term for this is 'stakeholder capitalism' and we think its time has come" (Hunt, Simpson, & Yamada 2020: 2).

The causes of MSV's demise build the case that MSV failed to deliver on its core promise of maximizing shareholder wealth, while also contributing to social inequities:

☐ Bill George led Medtronic, a leading healthcare device company, with capitalization from $1 billion to $60 billion in just over ten years, while growing revenues annually at 18 percent and earnings at 22 percent. George stated: "Contrary to what the advocates of maximizing short-term shareholder value would have us believe, the best kept-secret in business is that mission-driven companies create far more shareholder value than do financially driven firms" (2003: 61).

☐ MSV distributed profits to executives but not to workers. From 1978 to 2013, worker pay increased only 10 percent, while CEO pay increased 937 percent (Sisodia 2018). Shareholder ideology has contributed to a "drastic shift in gain sharing away from workers toward corporate elites, with stockholders and top management eating more of the economic pie" (Mayer, Strine, & Winter 2020).

☐ MSV funneled profits to shareholders at the expense of long-term invest-ment. Beginning in the late 1970s, the prevailing retain-and-reinvest approach of major US corporations changed to one of downsize and distribute (Lazonick 2015: 2). From 2003 to 2011, 54 percent of profits went to share buybacks (thus boosting share prices) and 37 percent went to dividends, while only 9 percent of was reinvested (Lazonick 2014: 4).

☐ MSV ideology considers the direct and indirect effects of capitalism as "externalities" outside of companies' responsibility. Business Roundtable's new purpose statement declares: "It is clear that this narrow, stockholder-centered view of corporations has cost society severely. . . . The single-minded focus of business on profits was criticized for causing the degradation of nature and biodiversity, contributing to global warming, stagnating wages, and exacerbating economic inequality" (Business Roundtable 2019).

MSV Is a Flawed Business Metric

MSV's central assertion is that capitalism is about maximizing shareholder wealth. Implicit is that shareholder wealth is the best metric for business success as it purports to be simple, objective, and accurate. However, the shareholder value metric is flawed in numerous ways. Here are four.

First, the value of a share at any given moment is an amalgam of countless subjective and extraneous inputs, including expectations of others' expect-ations. It is less objective and reliable than, say, using a patient's temperature as a valid indicator of their health, diagnosis, and prognosis. The "efficient market hypothesis" has not been upheld (Stout 2012: 65). A corporation's health, performance, and prospects surely do not rise or fall in tandem with the increasingly frequent and massive market swings.

Second, MSV ideology is grounded in the view of corporations being owned by shareholders ("principals") and managed by boards and executives ("agents"). This view states that shareholders are the principals because they own the corporation. Corporation ownership is not a simple issue, however; a strong argument can be made that corporations own themselves, removing a core pillar from the MSV edifice. The ownership issue aside, actual practice does not conform to the principal/agent theory. Boards and executives do not act as obedient servants to their shareholding "owners." Shareholders, as owners/principals, should be the ones paying their "servant" agents, yet, in practice, the opposite happens. Corporate boards set compensation for the "agents," who often handpick board members. Shareholders typically lack the agency to influence strategic decisions made by their "agents." They often find it difficult to oppose short-term transactions that may temporarily raise the share price while jeopardizing the long-term health of their companies. Shareholders often find it daunting just to get their issues on the agendas of "shareholder" meetings.

Third, many shareholders are not invested in the success of the companies in which they own shares. In 1960, the share turnover ratio on the New York Stock Exchange was 12 percent (the average share being held for about eight years). In 1987, share turnover rose to 73 percent. In 2010, the turnover rate was 300 percent. Today's turnover rate is difficult to estimate, but it has almost certainly increased since 2010 (Stout 2012: 66). Compare the "switching costs" of trading stocks for a typical shareholder today to the "switching costs" facing a sixty-year-old employee with thirty years of longevity, working for the only company in the area, which decides to shut down operations to increase profits even by a small margin. For MSV ideology, this asymmetry is acceptable.

Fourth, MSV ideology posits the maximization of just one element as a goal, as though that element existed independently, versus being just one element enmeshed in a complex, dynamic system. In a dynamic system, the variability of one component impacts the relationships among all other elements. Striving to maximize the benefits of the natural ecosystem just for butterflies is not a sound idea.

The immediate implosion of the proposed football Super League is an example of the costs of neglecting the ecosystem in which all businesses exist. As Sarah Keohane Williamson (2021) put it, "The Super League is a clear example of what can go wrong when there is an overemphasis on ownership rights without a recognition of broader responsibilities, and the costs to shareholders . . . recognizing stakeholder interests is critical to creating value over the long term – and taking them for granted is an easy way to destroy it."

Sustaining MSV ideology was a conceptual absurdity, an empirical impossibility, and a moral tragedy. In the long term, shareholders are negatively impacted if workers are without employment, work without a livable wage, cannot afford health insurance, receive poor schooling, or live in fractured families, disintegrating communities, and degrading physical environments. The "Tragedy of the Commons" is presented as a sad fact of life, not as a necessary corollary of a flawed idea. The common good is not an "externality" beyond the purview and responsibility of business. The MSV view is the true tragedy.

MSV Ideology Is a Culture

All social groups, such as those committed to MSV, develop shared outlooks and ideologies, that is, cultures. They bond through shared artifacts, values, and attitudes; behavioral norms; and deeply held assumptions.

The artifacts are the observable physical manifestations of culture (e.g., balance sheets, dividends, shares, and high CEO pay). The culture's values, attitudes, behavioral norms, and assumptions can be observed and inferred through the choices a culture's adherents consistently make (e.g., prioritizing short-term shareholder wealth and paying workers minimum wages, while paying executives richly and neglecting the common good).

These cultural manifestations may appear to be inconsistent and irrational. However, when the deep, underlying assumptions are uncovered, we see how cultural features make sense *in the minds of the culture members*. Culture members are typically not conscious of their deep assumptions, yet these assumptions drive the culture members' thinking, attitudes, and behaviors with uncanny consistency and fierce emotional attachment.

The reason for the consistency and attachment is that the deep assumptions do not emerge independently from one another. They emerge from one powerful, synthesizing view, a "root metaphor," of the world as a whole (Hayes, Hayes, & Reese 1988: 98). To understand the essence of a culture, one needs to identify its root metaphor and the comprising deep assumptions. *MSV's root metaphor is "avarice," which may be defined as extreme greed for material gain.* In other words, "I have the right to acquire as much as I can, without due regard for others." MSV's root metaphor comprises these deep assumptions, which mischaracterize humans and human life:

- Humans are primarily economic creatures (versus meaning-making creatures).
- Humans are essentially individual entities (rather than inherently interdependent).
- Humans are primarily propelled by self-interest to seek happiness defined as material gain (as opposed to also having interests and commitments beyond the self).
- Human life is essentially competitive (versus cooperative).
- The good of pursuing material gain takes precedence over other goods including the well-being of human and natural ecosystems.

Driven by MSV ideology's root metaphor, MSV's adherents created an ideological edifice that is conceptually incoherent, empirically flawed, and harmful to the world's ecosystems.

Why Does MSV Ideology Continue as a Zombie Idea?

Business Roundtable's new declaration of purpose signaled a significant ideological shift but has resulted in little tangible change. This was likely disappointing only to those who do not comprehend the power of culture. Deeply held beliefs and habits die hard. Strongly held assumptions remain unexamined.

MSV's core metaphor, deep assumptions, and the MSV metric still shape the thoughts, values, and actions of the great majority of the boards and CEOs of our largest corporations. Changing one's mindset from the singular goal of business as being to maximize shareholder wealth to that of enhancing the well-being of all stakeholders is a paradigm shift, not an incremental mental or operational adjustment. The required paradigm shift is not just cognitive. It also entails values. MSV ideology continues to serve the (short-term) self-interest of boards, CEOs, hedge funds, and day traders.

The cultural artifacts of MSV ideology constitute a powerful subsystem of their own: the quarterly earnings machinery, corporate governance and valuation, financial regulations, massive CEO compensation, and the courts. Dominant business and law school curricula also continue to promulgate MSV ideology. It would be futile to attempt to transform these cultural artifacts piecemeal without transforming the cultural engine that drives them.

Confusion Surrounding US Corporate Law

One place to start would be to reduce confusion regarding corporate governance law, particularly in the United States. This confusion works against moving away from MSV ideology.

In 2011, the Brookings Institution surveyed the teachings of leading US law and business schools on corporate purpose, law, and governance. Brookings' research concluded: "It appears that some law and business professors are mistakenly training future lawyers and corporate leaders that corporations have no authority to do good or benefit society other than its shareholders" (West 2011: 18). Lynn Stout (2012: 25), however, states: "The notion that corporate law requires directors, executives and employees to maximize shareholder wealth simply isn't true. . . . The idea is fable."

Given such uncertainty, many corporate fiduciary officers have osmosed the view that in *all* their decisions they must show that they have diligently striven to advance the financial interests of shareholders, even if other stakeholders are significantly harmed. US corporate law now offers a clear alternative, so that business leaders do not have to worry about breaching corporate law if they pursue goals that benefit all stakeholders.

Currently, thirty-seven US states have enacted "constituency statutes" that allow or even require corporate fiduciaries to take stakeholder interests into account. These statutes permit the formation of a "Public Benefit Corporation"

(PBC) (or just "Benefit Corporation"). PBCs are allowed (or required) to consider the legitimate interests and claims of *all* stakeholders.

The legal ground is rapidly shifting regarding how corporate officers can show that they have fulfilled their fiduciary duties. Given the strong evidence that MSV ideology delivers inferior value to shareholders and is inimical to long-term corporate health, corporate fiduciary officers ought now to demonstrate their good faith, care, and loyalty by adopting a governance model that optimizes sustainable returns for all stakeholders.

Reinventing Capitalism Is Well Underway

Jettisoning MSV will be difficult. Fortunately, however, a more humane version of capitalism has always existed. As MSV capitalism has disappointed and caused harm, this "human flourishing" form of capitalism has experienced a renaissance over the past twenty years. It goes by several names, including Conscious Capitalism and Inclusive Capitalism. I suggest we use the term "Purposeful All-Stakeholder" (PAS) capitalism, as it expresses the notion that stakeholder management ought to be imbued with purposes worthy of all stakeholders.

The various forms of Purposeful All-Stakeholder capitalism stem from a common root metaphor: Humans are social beings who seek meaning and purpose. The assumptions comprise:

- Humans have goals and interests that go beyond the self.
- Humans care about the true, the good, and the beautiful, not merely the material.
- Humans want to self-actualize – they want to develop their intellectual, psychological, moral, physical, and vocational capacities.
- Humans are enmeshed with each other and with nature – they want to contribute to their communities and to the common good.

The governing idea is that business life is a *fully human* endeavor that should be shaped by what helps humans, and our human and natural ecosystems, to flourish.

Purposeful All-Stakeholder companies follow a similar recipe that stems from their shared root metaphor and deep assumptions. These are their key ingredients that together create a beneficent cycle:

- A worthy purpose that inspires all stakeholders.
- Genuine caring for their employees, who are carefully selected, highly trained, well-compensated, and treated with respect.

- Employees become more deeply engaged; learn more and perform better; treat customers very well; turn over less; and become ambassadors for their company.
- Delighted customers spend more and are more loyal, resulting in free advertising and less marketing; customers become brand ambassadors.
- Gross margins run smaller, with revenues heavily invested in employees, products, and operations; profits are steady, reinvested in the company, and shared with employees and community.

Adherents of the "human flourishing" model consistently outperform MSV companies. BlackRock CEO Larry Fink (2021) noted the superior performance of purposeful companies in his 2021 Letter to CEOs:

> Over the course of 2020, we have seen how purposeful companies with better environmental, social, and governance (ESG) profiles, have outperformed their peers. During 2020, 81% of a globally representative selection of sustainable indexes outperformed their parent benchmarks. This outperformance was even more pronounced during the first quarter downturn, another instance of sustainable funds' resilience that we have seen in prior downturns.

In addition to the many businesses listed in Fink's sustainable indices referenced in his 2021 letter, established PAS companies include Costco, the world's fifth-largest retailer, with over 800 stores in 11 countries, 100 million members, and 275,000 employees worldwide. In 2020, its revenues exceeded $163 billion, and earnings exceeded $4 billion (Costco 2021). The company limits its wholesale markup to a maximum of 15 percent, passing along that value to its customers.

Costco's starting pay is $16 per hour, with over half the employees earning more than $25 per hour. Most Costco employees also receive bonuses totaling up to $4,000 annually. Costco's healthcare benefits are generous, with 89 percent of employees being eligible and 97 percent of those eligible enrolled. The company's employee turnover rate is 13 percent overall, falling to just 6 percent for employees who stay more than one year (the retail industry average is about 60 percent) (Jelinek 2021). Costco's average sales per square foot is $1,250, compared with Sam's Club's $725. Its inventory turnover rate is approximately 30 percent higher than Walmart's (simplysafedividends.com 2019). Since going public thirty-five years ago, Costco stock has generated a compound annual growth rate (CAGR) of approximately 16.7 percent, excluding dividends. Over the same period, the S&P 500 generated a CAGR of about 8.3 percent (Patel 2020).

The "Firms of Endearment" (FoEs) are twenty-two US public firms, twenty-nine private firms, and fifteen non-US firms that "are fueled by passion and purpose" and "endear themselves to stakeholders by bringing the interests of all stakeholders into strategic alignment." The FoEs' cumulative investment performance over fifteen years (1996–2011) was 1,646 percent, while the S&P 500's performance was 157 percent (Sisodia, Sheth, & Wolfe 2014: 20)

In 2021, multinational consumer giant leaders Jonas Samuelson (CEO, Electrolux, 48,000+ employees), Stanislas de Gramont (COO, Groupe SEB, 25,985 employees), and Carsten Olesen (president Consumer Audio, Harman International, 30,000+ employees) fully affirmed the PAS model, rejecting MSV as "old school thinking" (Joly 2021). These and thousands of other PAS firms have discovered what has been hiding in plain sight: Treating stakeholders with genuine respect and care sustains business success and adds quality to our common life. Hubert Joly, who turned around Best Buy from near-bankruptcy, declares: "I have come to believe – to know – that *purpose* and *human connections* – constitute the very heart of business. And I believe they should be at the heart of the very necessary and urgent refoundation of business now underway" (Joly & Lambert 2021: 4).

Changing an entrenched ideology is difficult yet also imperative. As BlackRock CEO Larry Fink (2021) states:

> Business leaders and boards will need to show great courage and commitment to their stakeholders. We need to move even faster – to create more jobs, more prosperity, and more inclusivity. . . . As we move forward from the pandemic, facing tremendous economic pain and inequality, we need companies to embrace a form of capitalism that recognizes and serves all their stakeholders.

4 Innovation and Financialization in the Corporate Economy
William Lazonick

Innovative Enterprise

Through investment in productive capabilities by governments, businesses, and households, a nation can achieve stable and equitable growth. A nation needs productivity growth to have the possibility of raising its population's living standards. It wants employment to be stable over time so that households that send members into the paid labor force have dependable streams of income over decades of work. A nation should want the revenues that a business corporation generates to be equitably shared among its "stakeholders," reflecting their contributions to creating the value that has enabled its productivity growth.

Conventional economic and political analyses that view the operation and performance of the economy in terms of the interaction of "states and markets" are ill-suited to comprehend the determinants of stable and equitable growth. Missing from this perspective is the role of the large-scale business corporation as the economy's central resource allocator. In the United States, 2017 data indicates that 2,156 firms with 5,000 or more US-based employees (and an average of 20,859) made up just 0.04 percent of all firms but employed 35 percent of the business-sector labor force. Moreover, these firms accounted for 40 percent of business-sector payrolls and 45 percent of revenues (United States Census Bureau 2021). The resource allocation decisions made by the executives who exercise strategic control over these very large firms have profound impacts on employment opportunity, income distribution, and productivity growth in the US economy.

In general, a firm grows to become a large-scale employer by generating one or more products that are higher quality and lower cost than those of its competitors in the markets that it serves. In a word, "innovation" drives the growth of the firm. Firm-level innovation requires strategy, organization, and finance (Lazonick 2019). Senior executives who exercise *strategic control* over the firm's resource allocation make strategic decisions about the products and processes in which to invest. The implementation of the innovation strategy requires the *organizational integration* of numerous people with different hierarchical responsibilities and functional specialties into the firm-level learning processes that are the essence of innovation. The firm must secure *financial commitment* to sustain the innovation process until, through transforming technologies and accessing markets, it can create the higher-quality, lower-cost products that, through market sales, generate financial returns.

Three *social conditions of innovative enterprise* – strategic control, organizational integration, and financial commitment – must interact to enable a business firm to generate an innovative (i.e., higher-quality, lower-cost) product. Those executives who exercise strategic control must have the abilities and incentives to allocate resources to innovation processes. Organizational integration provides employees with the abilities (through workforce training and work experience) and incentives (through pay increases and career opportunities) to implement the firm's innovation strategy. Financial commitment enables the firm to invest in the "dynamic capabilities" (Teece 2009), embodied in the skills and efforts of its labor force, that are required to generate innovative outcomes.

Innovative enterprise, characterized by the dynamic interaction of strategic control, organizational integration, and financial commitment, does not occur in a social vacuum. As displayed in Figure 1, national institutions related to governance, employment, and investment shape and are shaped by the social conditions of innovative enterprise that prevail in that nation's leading business corporations. Governance institutions define the rights and responsibilities of those who exercise strategic control over resource allocation. Employment institutions determine the education of the labor force and the general terms of management–worker relations. Investment institutions structure the flow of finance for investment in the nation's productive capabilities.

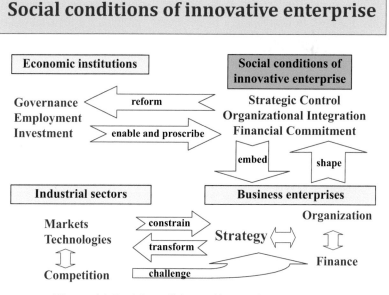

Figure 4.1 Social conditions of innovative enterprise

As indicated in the "social conditions" schematic, industrial sectors (or subsectors) in which firms are engaged differ in terms of technologies, markets, and competition. Technologies are combinations of physical capital and human capabilities. High-tech companies seek to measure investment in organizational learning in terms of R&D expenditures, but the enhancement of human capabilities that enable innovation can occur throughout the firm, in functions such as manufacturing, purchasing, and marketing. In 2018, of the 500 very large companies included in the S&P 500 Index, 38 firms accounted for 75 percent of all R&D expenditures while 382 firms recorded no R&D expenses at all.[5] Yet many of these "non-R&D" companies have grown large through innovation based on organizational learning.

Markets differ in terms of quality demanded, incomes and numbers of potential buyers, and buyers' price elasticity of demand. For any product, there are many dimensions of quality. In the passenger-car industry, for example, "high quality" may mean that that a car is safe, fuel efficient, and environmentally friendly – dimensions of quality that are of public concern and are hence often subject to government regulation. It may also mean that the car is rust resistant, air-conditioned, roomy, stylish, comfortable, etc. – quality dimensions that are left to consumer choice. It costs money to build quality into cars, and different types of government regulators and car buyers may register very different views about what "high quality" means and how much it should cost to attain.

Within an industrial sector, firms compete with one another in terms of quality and cost. In developing a higher-quality product, the innovating firm incurs the fixed cost of investments not only in physical capital (plant and equipment) but also in human capabilities (enhanced through organizational learning). The amount of fixed cost incurred in developing a higher-quality product depends on both the size and the duration of the innovative investment strategy. If the size of investment in physical capital tends to increase the fixed cost of an innovation strategy, so too does the duration of the investment required for the firm to engage in the collective and cumulative – or organizational – learning central to an innovation process that can transform technologies and access markets.

An innovation strategy that can eventually develop a higher-quality product may place the innovating firm at a competitive disadvantage when it has only attained low output levels. The high fixed cost of an innovation strategy creates the need for the firm to attain a high level of utilization of the productive capabilities it has developed and thus reap "economies of scale." Given its

---

[5] Author's calculations based on S&P Compustat database.

existing productive capabilities, the innovating firm may experience increasing costs of variable inputs that it buys as needed on the market to expand production. To overcome this constraint on its innovation strategy, the innovating firm integrates the production of the supply of that input into its internal operations. The development of the productive capability of this newly integrated input, however, adds to the fixed cost of the innovation strategy. The innovating firm is now under even more pressure to expand its sold output to transform high fixed cost into low unit cost.

When a firm develops productive capabilities to gain competitive advantage in one line of business, it can make use of those capabilities to transform technologies and access markets in related lines of business – and hence grow by becoming a multiproduct firm. The critical decisions concerning which new business lines to enter depend on the abilities and incentives of executives in positions of strategic control. By providing career opportunities within the firm to key employees whom the company wants to retain, the growth of the multiproduct firm relies upon, and can strengthen, organizational integration. And the profits from successful innovation provide the firm with financial commitment in the form of retained earnings that can be used to reward career employees for their contributions to prior innovation and invest in augmenting the productive capabilities required for the next generation of innovative products.

Corporate Financialization

In short, the innovative firm grows through a strategy of "retain and reinvest": It retains both profits and people and reinvests in productive capabilities. As a result, the innovative firm contributes to stable and equitable growth. But the firm's innovative success creates the possibility that its strategy can turn from retain and reinvest to "downsize and distribute": It can downsize its labor force and distribute corporate cash to shareholders in the form of dividends and stock buybacks. Rather than invest in productive capabilities to enable further innovation, the firm seeks to cut costs and inflate profits so that it can use its cash flow to increase yields to shareholders. As an intermediate stage, the previously innovative firm can reorient its resource allocation to a strategy of "dominate and distribute": It can continue to grow in the business lines that it has come to dominate but use its profits to increase yields to shareholders via income streams in the form of dividends as well as manipulative boosts to the company's stock price by large-scale stock buybacks done as open-market repurchases.

The strategic reorientation of the firm from retain and reinvest to downsize and distribute by way of dominate and distribute represents a transformation from innovation to financialization. The result, as evidenced by the increasing financialization of the US corporate economy since the 1980s, is unstable employment opportunity, inequitable income distribution, and sagging productivity growth. Stock buybacks represent the foremost method of "predatory value extraction": the power of certain parties to extract value from a firm that is far greater than their contributions to the firm's value creation. In *Predatory Value Extraction* (Lazonick & Shin 2020), I analyze how, since the 1980s on a generally increasing scale, senior executives as value-extracting insiders, asset-fund managers as value-extracting enablers, and corporate raiders as value-extracting outsiders have, in combination, engaged in legalized looting of the US business corporation.

As a form of distribution to shareholders, buybacks done as open-market repurchases are much more volatile than dividends, with buybacks booming when stock prices are high. Since the early 1980s, major US business corporations have been doing buybacks in addition to paying dividends. For 1981–3, the 216 companies in the S&P 500 Index in January 2020 that were publicly listed for 1981–2019 distributed 49.7 percent of net income as dividends but only 4.4 percent as buybacks. For 2017–19, dividends were 49.6 percent of net income but buybacks for the same 216 companies were 62.2 percent.[6]

Both types of distributions to shareholders drain corporate treasuries, but they differ in terms of how gains from them are realized. Dividends provide all shareholders with a yield on *holding* shares. In contrast, buybacks done as open-market repurchases (the vast majority of buybacks) increase the gains of *share-sellers* who, as professional stock traders, are in the business of timing the sale of the shares that they hold, as they benefit from access to nonpublic information on the precise days on which the company is executing buybacks. These privileged sharesellers include senior executives of the company doing the buybacks, Wall Street bankers, and hedge fund managers.

Stable shareholders who buy corporate stocks for dividend yields should be opposed to buybacks. Instead, they should want corporate management to reinvest in the productive capabilities of the company as a basis for creating the next round of innovative products that can generate the profits out of which a stream of dividends can continue to be paid. If the firm is successful in making these innovative investments, the shares of the company will rise in value, giving these shareholders a stock price gain if and when they decide to sell some or all of their shares.

Why, then, are companies making these massive distributions to shareholders? The short answer is Rule 10b-18, adopted by the US Securities and

---

[6] Author's calculations based on S&P Compustat database.

Exchange Commission (SEC) in 1982, which provides publicly listed corporations with a "safe harbor" against charges of stock price manipulation, even when they do hundreds of millions of dollars in buybacks, trading day after trading day. In aggregate, for 2019–20, companies in the S&P 500 Index did $5.3 trillion in buybacks, equivalent to 54 percent of combined net income, and another $3.8 trillion in dividends, 39 percent of net income.[7]

Table 4.1 shows the twenty-five largest stock repurchasers for the decade 2010–19 among US industrial (i.e., nonfinancial) corporations. These twenty-five companies did $1.8 trillion in buybacks during 2010–19 and accounted for 34 percent of all buybacks by companies in the S&P 500 Index. Of these twenty-five companies, sixteen distributed more than 100 percent of net income to shareholders over the decade while another six distributed 80 percent or more. Alphabet is a special retain-and-reinvest case because it does buybacks to support the stock price of its nonvoting Class C shares, which it uses for stock-based employee compensation and has available for stock-based acquisitions. As for the other twenty-four companies, suffice it to state here that those currently in dominate-and-distribute mode are Apple, Oracle, Microsoft, Cisco, Walmart, Intel, Home Depot, Johnson & Johnson, Qualcomm, Amgen, Disney, Gilead Sciences, Lowe's, Comcast, and Coca-Cola, while those in downsize-and-distribute mode are Exxon Mobil, IBM, Pfizer, Procter & Gamble, General Electric, Hewlett-Packard (now two companies), Merck, McDonald's, and Boeing.[8]

While SEC Rule 10b-18 permits these massive buybacks, the ideology that, for the sake of efficiency, companies should be run to "maximize shareholder value" (MSV) has legitimized them since the 1980s. The MSV argument, put forth by academic economists known as agency theorists, is that, of all of a company's participants, it is only shareholders who allocate resources to the firm without a guaranteed return and, hence, it is only shareholders who have a claim on the firm's profits, if and when they occur. Agency theory thus legitimizes downsize and distribute, positing that by "disgorging" the firm's "free" cash flow to shareholders, the economy's productive resources will be allocated to their best alternative uses (Lazonick & Shin 2020).

In making this shareholder-primacy argument, however, agency theory lacks a theory of innovative enterprise (TIE) and hence provides no explanation of how "best alternative uses" come to exist. The theory explains how households as taxpayers (through government investment in physical infrastructure and

---

[7] Author's calculations based on S&P Compustat database.

[8] Studies of many of these companies and the damage that buybacks do are available at www .ineteconomics.org/research/experts/wlazonick/, https://hbr.org/search?term=william+lazonick/, and https://theairnet.org.

Table 4.1 Twenty-five largest stock repurchasers for the decade 2010–19 among US industrial corporations

$BB RANK	COMPANY	BUYBACKS 2010–19 ($billions)	BB/NI%	DV/NI%	(BB+DV)/ NI%
1	APPLE	305.0	76	21	94
2	ORACLE	118.7	127	24	151
3	MICROSOFT	113.0	54	44	98
4	EXXON MOBIL	92.4	35	45	80
5	IBM	89.2	72	37	108
6	CISCO SYSTEMS	85.9	106	44	150
7	PFIZER	76.7	60	55	116
8	WALMART	70.2	50	41	91
9	INTEL	67.9	52	36	88
10	HOME DEPOT	64.4	93	45	137
11	JOHNSON & JOHNSON	62.1	49	62	110
12	QUALCOMM	55.1	133	59	192
13	PROCTER & GAMBLE	54.9	52	64	117
14	ALPHABET	52.2	31	0	31
15	AMGEN	51.6	93	37	130
16	GENERAL ELECTRIC	50.3	135	179	313
17	HEWLETT-PACKARD*	48.6	128	31	159
18	DISNEY	47.8	61	24	85
19	MERCK	45.8	81	91	172
20	MCDONALD'S	45.8	87	58	145
21	BOEING	43.5	88	50	138
22	GILEAD SCIENCES	39.6	56	19	75
23	LOWE'S	35.6	135	37	172
24	COMCAST	35.6	38	23	62
25	COCA-COLA	35.0	46	73	119
	25 COMPANIES COMBINED	1,786.9	65	40	106

Note: BB – stock buybacks, DV – cash dividends, NI – net income. * Data are for Hewlett-Packard, 2010–15, plus HP Inc. and Hewlett-Packard Enterprise, combined 2016–19.
Source: Author's calculations based on S&P Compustat database.

human capabilities) and workers (through their value-creating employment) make productive contributions to the firm's profits without guaranteed returns.

No matter the corporate tax rate, households as taxpayers face the risk that technological, market, and competitive uncertainties may prevent enterprises from generating profits and the related business tax revenues that serve as a return on government investments in infrastructure and capabilities. Moreover, corporate tax rates are politically determined. Households as taxpayers face the political uncertainty that, armed with MSV ideology, predatory value extractors may convince government policymakers that they will not be able to make value-creating investments unless the corporations are given tax cuts or financial subsidies that will permit higher after-tax profits.

Through their skills and efforts, workers regularly make productive contributions to the companies for which they work that are beyond the levels required to lay claim to their current pay. They do so, however, without guaranteed returns. An innovative company wants workers who apply their skills and efforts to organizational learning so that they can make productive contributions. For their part, workers expect that they will be able to build their careers with the company, putting themselves in positions to reap future benefits at work and in retirement. Yet these potential careers and returns are not guaranteed. In fact, under the downsize-and-distribute resource-allocation regime that MSV ideology legitimizes, these careers and the returns from them are generally undermined.

Therefore, workers supply their skills and efforts to innovation processes that could create value if successful, but they take the risk that their endeavors could be in vain. Far from reaping expected gains in the form of higher earnings and superior in-house career opportunities, workers could face cuts in pay and benefits, or even find themselves laid off, if the firm's innovative investment strategy fails. Even if the innovation process is successful, workers face the possibility that the institutional environment in which MSV prevails will empower corporate executives to cut some workers' wages and lay off other workers – and distribute the value that these employees helped to create as dividends and buybacks to shareholders.

MSV ignores the risk–reward relation for households as taxpayers and workers in the operation and performance of business corporations. The irony of MSV is that public shareholders typically never invest in the value-creating capabilities of the company at all. Rather, they purchase outstanding corporate equities with the expectation that dividend income (where applicable) will be forthcoming while they hold the shares and that, if and when they decide to sell the shares, they will be able to reap stock price gains. In SEC-sanctioned stock buybacks, senior corporate executives possess a powerful tool for giving that "capital gain" a manipulative boost – and in the process, as I summed it up in an article published in *Harvard Business Review* in 2014, "make most Americans worse off" (Lazonick 2014).

Reforming Economic Institutions to Suppress Financialization and Promote Innovation

Guided by the "social conditions of innovative enterprise" perspective, the United States can transition from a value-extracting economy, characterized by extreme inequality, to a value-creating economy, characterized by stable and equitable growth, through a five-part agenda to reform its governance, employment, and investment institutions (Lazonick & Shin 2020: ch. 8):

☐ Ban stock buybacks by rescinding SEC Rule 10b-18.

☐ Compensate senior executives for their contributions to value creation, not value extraction.

☐ Reconstitute corporate boards by including directors representing workers and taxpayers.

☐ Reform the corporate tax system so that it recognizes and supports corporate investments in enhancing productive capabilities.

☐ Deploy corporate profits and government taxes to collaborations between government agencies and business firms that support the lifelong-learning careers of members of the US labor force.

5 Corporate Governance, CEO Compensation, and the Income Gap

Arie Y. Lewin and Till Talaulicar

Introduction

The practice of corporate governance has undergone striking changes as the direct agency between shareholders and corporate management has weakened. Individual shareholders have become largely disconnected from the monitoring of top management, and the capital markets have witnessed the growth and influence of financial intermediaries, such as mutual funds, hedge funds, equity funds, and retirement funds, whose goals may not align with those whose funds they manage. In many liberal democratic economies, this has led to the visible concentration of wealth and power in an increasingly small corporate elite and perceived inequalities in wealth creation and income distribution. This section focuses on the role of corporate governance in these outcomes, particularly the interplay between the board compensation committee and the CEO. We argue that management is motivated to maximize personal wealth during its tenure, with the consequence of favoring short-termism over long-term investments in the growth of the corporation (and the economy).

In the wake of the globalization of capital markets, the doctrine of maximizing shareholder value (MSV) has gained adherents across the world. But it became largely disconnected from monitoring management (see Section 3). Numerous reforms of governance systems have been enacted to strengthen the orientation of the enterprise toward the interests of its shareholders. Three decades of governance reforms, however, have proved to be inadequate to forestall adverse outcomes. The worldwide financial market crisis, as well as mounting concerns with distributive justice and other societal challenges, have given rise to questions about the legitimacy of capitalism as we know it today, potentially undermining the long-term viability of the business system (see Section 1).

A key concern is a growing level of income inequality. There is mounting evidence that inequality has increased (Piketty 2014). Lazonick (2019) noted that between 1970 and 2020 productivity increased by 243.6 percent while hourly compensation increased by only 114.7 percent. This contrasts with the period 1950–73 when productivity increased by 95.7 percent and hourly compensation by 90.9 percent.

Whereas some levels of economic inequality may be acceptable (Haack & Sieweke 2018), justified (Prasad 2018), or even desirable for strengthening incentives (Agarwal & Holmes 2019), the perceptions of excessive levels of inequality in income and wealth may be sufficient to engender a crisis of capitalism that directs attention to weaknesses and inadequacies of corporate governance practices. As Tsui, Enderle, and Jiang (2018: 156) admonished:

> "Extreme income inequality challenges all economies, both developed and developing, by causing social inequality, bringing misery to those at the bottom and power and influence to those at the top, dividing the minority 'haves' from the majority 'have-nots,' allowing the powerful to create conditions that further increase their wealth, and causing the deprived to become poorer."

CEO compensation is indicative of the steep rise in the gap between the compensation package of the highest corporate executives and the average paid members of the firm (de Vaan, Elbers, & DiPrete 2019). Agency theory underlies the evolving logic of appropriateness (March & Olsen 2011), relating to the alignment of long-term shareholder value with management's personal goals, specifically due to the application of stock grants as an integral part of the compensation package. But there is no evidence that the system leading to exorbitant and headline-grabbing pay packets can self-correct.

CEO Pay and Firm Performance

Aligning the interests of executives with the interests of the owners has been mainly addressed by establishing pay-for-performance compensation plans. However, in practice CEO compensation (including realized stock options) over the period 1978–2018 grew at least 25 percent faster than the value of the stock market (Mishel & Wolfe 2019). Executive compensation levels that have been perceived to be excessive have instigated government responses and governance reforms intended to address such CEO compensation packages (Borisova, Salas, & Zagorchev 2019).

The compensation committee of the board of directors is responsible for recommending to the board the compensation package for the CEO (Sun & Cahan 2012). The underlying model governing the committee assumes that it acts as a risk-neutral agent that is able to design an optimal CEO compensation package that optimizes CEO incentives and aligns them with shareholder interests.

Although the CEO pay–performance relationship is assumed to be at the core of the principal–agent theory, extant studies basically report weak or no relationships between CEO compensation and firm performance (Bebchuk & Fried 2004). The empirical literature on compensation committee effectiveness does not directly address how the CEO and other top executives are able to mitigate the moral hazard problem associated with equity-based bonuses.

Some researchers have argued that the CEO or the top executive team have the information power to both influence the financial goals for the next fiscal year and extract rents for themselves that negatively affect long-term shareholder value (e.g., Bebchuk, Fried, & Walker 2002). Other empirical findings provide weak support (in terms of effect size) that inside directors, aligned with the CEO (Conyon & Peck 1998) and the CEOs of other firms serving on the board, support compensation packages favored by the CEO (e.g., Westphal & Zajac 1997).

Graham, Harvey, and Rajgopal (2005) document that executives neglect long-term value in order to hit short-term earnings per share (EPS) targets. Top management routinely sacrifice shareholder value to meet earnings expectations and smooth reported earnings. There is evidence of the widespread use of "real" earnings management, which might include deferring a valuable project or slashing R&D expenditures to meet quarterly earning consensus forecasts.

Management Motivation to Maximize Personal Wealth

Williamson (1963) developed a theory of why and how managers are motivated to maximize personal wealth earned or extracted from their corporate employer. The core assumption is that managers are motivated to maximize personal wealth subject to maintaining their membership in the organization. The means for maximizing salary increases and bonuses is to maximize control over discretionary resources, what Cyert and March (1963) called "organization slack." Schiff and Lewin (1968, 1970, 1974) demonstrated how the annual strategic planning and budget process allows managers to extract resources. During the annual budget–financial planning process the organization is in a temporary state of quasi-conflict resolution. Schiff and Lewin (1968, 1974) observed that during the budget planning process commitments are made that affect revenue goals, including new products and incremental enhancements to products and services as well as detailed cost commitments and planned operational efficiencies across all organizational units. Although the annual budget process is intense and time consuming, it is also quite predictable, at least in its usual format, since the aspiration for any budget item for the next fiscal year is based on what the aspiration was in the previous budget, the actual aspiration that was achieved, and the experience of a comparison group (e.g., competitors). Most of the give-and-take is about the increase in commitments extracted for every organizational unit. In a large corporation with multiple business units this process is repeated within each business unit and then aggregated at the corporate level. Schiff and Lewin (1968, 1970, 1974) described the process as underestimating revenue commitments and maximizing estimated costs. Financial analysts refer to this practice as "sand-bagging" (Steele & Albright 2004). Managers are engaged in "underpromising" in order to overdeliver and thus earn contingent salary increments and bonuses.

For large corporations, the annual strategic financial planning process allows management to absorb the uncertainty inherent in plans that are finalized fourteen to sixteen months out. Short of some unanticipated crisis such as the Black Monday stock market crash in 1987 or the recent COVID-19 pandemic, the aggregate operational goals of the firm are quite predictable. As the financial plans are realized, slack resources are expended. In the rare case that revenues fail to exceed the goals, management can still make the anticipated bottom line goals by holding off slack budget allocations (e.g., delaying new projects, avoiding staff increases, or introducing process efficiencies that create positive manufacturing variances). Over time, the long-term consequence is a subtle but real shift to short-termism – a focus on smoothing reported income because the market and the analysts rewarded predictable financial performance from quarter to quarter. Short-term decision-making became the logic of appropriateness for financial planning year on year. This privileges strategies based on prioritizing incremental (instead of radical) innovation and operational efficiencies, which can include the suppression of wages by exercising monopsony power in smaller markets and/or by outsourcing and offshoring.

The implication is that boards of directors and compensation committees share the expectation of analysts for smooth and predictable financial performance and that the design of CEO compensation packages reflects these priorities as well. Moreover, the CEO and the top management team have information power vis-à-vis the board and the compensation committee in negotiating financial goals for the next fiscal year and their compensation packages.

The extant literature on negotiating the compensation package is quite opaque, especially regarding the application of "comparability" routines for selecting benchmarking companies (Faulkender & Yang 2010). Much of this process is considered confidential and relies on compensation consultants (Murphy & Sandino 2019). However, the board of directors must formally approve the recommendations of the compensation committee.

Most publicly traded US companies design compensation packages that reward top managers for achieving or exceeding EPS targets (Edmans, Gabaix, & Jenter 2017). Over time, as a means of aligning managers' financial goals and the firms' long-term growth strategy, compensation committees began to increase the stock grant compensation component to the point that a mix of stock grants made up the entire compensation package. Preferential tax treatment for long-term capital gains also favors stock grants over cash salaries.

The use of stock as compensation resulted in various unanticipated problems. Lazonick (2014) observed a growing trend of companies conducting stock buybacks. He concluded that management motivation to monetize their stock grants became the driver to initiate stock buybacks. The underlying assumption is that stock buybacks will be beneficial to the EPS metric as they decrease the number of shares outstanding, which directly benefits managers monetizing their stock grants. However, they may also distort actual firm performance by diverting cash from long-term investments. If the compensation package does not exclude the effect of stock buybacks on EPS in bonus calculations, management will be incentivized to engage in stock buybacks (Cheng, Harford, & Zhang 2015), particularly if EPS forecasts would otherwise be missed (Almeida, Fos, & Kronlund 2016). The unparalleled increase in stock buybacks and the steep rise in top management stock grant compensation has given rise to perceptions of executive self-dealing through stock buybacks at the expense of investing in the long-term future of the enterprise (see Section 4).

Growing the scale of the enterprise through mergers and acquisitions is also related to compensation plans (Bodolica & Spraggon 2009). CEOs initiate and justify large acquisitions for strategic reasons, such as geographical diversification, economies of scale and scope, eliminating a competitor, decreased overhead costs, or increased margins – which strategically support varied competitive strategic reasoning. But growing scale also leads the compensation committee to reassess the compensation package of the CEO by applying the "comparability" rule to at least maintain peer parity. In addition, it is common to pay a cash bonus for successful acquisition outcomes (Grinstein & Hribar 2004). CEOs are hence rewarded for their deal-making activities (Fich, Starks, & Yore 2014). As with stock buybacks, growth through mergers and acquisitions benefits CEOs, consistent with Williamson's theory that managers are motivated to maximize their personal wealth while employed by their corporation.

Potential Remedies

Since the prevailing compensation schemes have been shown to foster short-term orientation and income inequality, potential avenues to overcome these shortcomings are sought. Due to the weak link between variable pay and performance, Frey and Osterloh (2005) have suggested that executives be paid a fixed salary, like bureaucrats. To reduce skewed income distributions, the publication of pay ratios that capture the pay gap between the CEO and the median employee have been proposed to assess and possibly limit the levels of executive compensation. However, their effects may be weak depending on the definition of the ratio – or even detrimental, because executives may seek to outsource less-qualified and lower-paid parts of their workforce (Edmans, Gabaix, & Jenter 2017).

An alternative approach is to hold executives accountable to a broader range of stakeholders. To overcome the deeply ingrained orientation toward shareholder value, a more diverse composition of the board that includes representatives of other stakeholders, most notably employees, has been suggested. Some countries, such as Germany, have mandatory regimes of codetermination according to which up to 50 percent of supervisory board members are representatives of the workforce of the firm. The effects of such arrangements, however, are ambiguous. For instance, Kim, Maug, and Schneider (2018) have demonstrated that board-level participation of the workforce tends to protect against layoffs but also to lower employee wages. Hence, the workforce pays for its implicit labor insurance without impacting the income of executives.

Regarding the design of compensation schemes, pay structures may need to be simplified, based on long-term equity and debt, and include long-term restricted stocks. The inclusion of nonfinancial performance measures in executive compensation plans may emphasize the importance of business goals beyond a narrow focus on shareholder returns. Moreover, they could promote a stronger focus on strategic activities and the long-term consequences of managerial courses of action. Tahir, Ibrahim, and Nurullah (2019) have shown that CEO bonus plans that include nonfinancial and long-term performance measures may encourage executives to work toward the long-term success of their firms, rather than their own short-term reward. Similarly, Flammer, Hong, and Minor (2019) have demonstrated that executive compensation packages that integrate criteria of corporate social responsibility increase long-term orientation and improve social performance. However, such compensation schemes need to be carefully designed and determined by the boards in order to avoid managerial misuse for manipulation or entrenchment as they may be open to gaming, similar to the budget sandbagging behavior discussed above.

CEO compensation will remain on the agenda of upcoming governance reforms. The increased awareness of its relation to the rising income gap has created additional attention to this theme. Compensation schemes need to motivate top management to focus on the long-term benefit of the enterprise and avoid the shortcomings of incentives that favor short-termism and ignore the interests of the various constituencies of the firm. Such schemes may also help to rebuild trust in the corporate sector and strengthen its legitimacy.

6 Reviving Productive Capitalism: How CEOs and Boards Can Drive Sustained Value Creation

Sarah Keohane Williamson

While capitalism has always been a subject of contention, the global financial crisis that took hold in 2007 brought the systemic problems in the large industrial economies into sharp relief.[9] The enhanced scrutiny came not only from domestic movements such as Occupy Wall Street, but also from the West's chief geopolitical rival, China, where President Xi Jinping took office in 2013 endorsing the Marxist formula that "capitalism is bound to die out and socialism is bound to win."[10] Social disorder over racial inequality and the initial mishandling of the COVID-19 pandemic in the West further strengthened China's argument that its model of authoritarian capitalism offers a stable alternative to countries that line up behind it.

Many of the problems leading to unsatisfactory outcomes in liberal democracies are external to individual firms. This includes the systemic forces that influence corporate decision-making. The finance sector has transformed itself from its traditional role in connecting investors with productive activity to encompass trading and other activities that generate short-term gains and fees. Large investors in the system with long-term interests, such as pension and mutual funds, can potentially provide a countervailing force but typically play only a passive role as company "owners." The COVID-19 pandemic has placed further short-term demands on executives, forcing many to postpone or end some long-term growth projects.

While this system has generated enormous wealth in the finance sector, it has created problems in the productive economy, such as greater concentration of firm size and fewer listings by startups (Lattanzio, Megginson, & Sanati 2021). Brilliant minds are drawn into the expanding financial sector and away from real-economy jobs. Cuts in research spending are too often rewarded as evidence of efficiency, and innovation activities are increasingly geared toward short-term applications. Labor productivity growth rates have declined in many developed countries since at least the late 1990s (Goldin et al. 2021).

Inside real-economy firms, managers are rewarded extravagantly for meeting a series of short-term targets even if this impairs potential growth in the long-term value of a company. In a 2003 survey of more than 300 corporate financial officers, 78 percent reported that they had sacrificed long-term value

[9] This section is adapted from Sneader et al. (2021).
[10] From a speech given shortly after Xi became general secretary, on January 5, 2013, to the Party's then–newly elected Central Committee (Greer 2019).

(e.g., by dropping potentially profitable investments) to smooth earnings (Graham, Campbell, & Rajgopal 2005). While top management has allied itself with the desires of the finance community, the labor share of national income in most developed economies has declined since the 1980s, with a steeper drop since 2000.

Ample evidence shows that companies create more value for investors when executives consistently make decisions and investments with long-term objectives in mind (e.g., Wang & Bansal 2012; Brauer 2013; Hoffmann, Wulf, & Stubner 2016; Barton et al. 2017; Flammer & Bansal 2017). This is consistent with the new push toward stakeholder primacy, because the interests of stakeholders and shareholders tend to converge in the long run: The firm won't prosper if its employees, customers, suppliers, and partners don't prosper. The future should belong to managers who have a long-term orientation and accept the importance of treating various stakeholders fairly.

Nevertheless, our research shows that behavior focused on short-term benefits has increased in recent years. An online survey conducted by McKinsey in June and July 2020, in which more than 400 executives participated, found a statistically significant increase in short-term behavior from 2015 to 2019.

There are many forces pushing managers toward short-term thinking. In addition to the quarterly focus of big investors, CEO compensation in most companies has been shown to more closely reflect short-term results, rather than long-term (ten-year) outcomes (Marshall 2017). Boards of directors are supposed to keep managers in line with shareholder interests, but a 2013 McKinsey survey of 772 directors found that only 22 percent believed their boards were completely aware of how their firms created value (Barton & Wiseman 2015).

Another reason executives may continue to focus on short-term results is that adopting a long-term orientation can be challenging. The practical aspects of managing for long-term performance are simply not well understood. This section summarizes the results of joint research that FCLTGlobal and McKinsey have undertaken to fill this gap. By synthesizing existing research in this area and the new online survey mentioned above, we found that companies with an eye on the long term adhere to five growth-promoting behaviors, as follows.

1. Invest sufficient capital and talent in large, risky initiatives

Many established businesses have developed an aversion to risky bets. Instead of playing to win, they play not to lose – and so they struggle to stay ahead of competitors. Companies that succeed in the long term identify strategic moves that will keep them ahead of trends in their industry. A prominent example is Microsoft's investment in "cloud computing" (data centers and associated services for use by other companies) in the 2010s. The company invested billions of dollars annually over many years building up a line of business for which it was not well known, but which by 2020 accounted for roughly a third of its revenue and an even higher percentage of its operating income.

Companies must commit sufficient resources to strategic initiatives such as product innovation, marketing and sales, and talent development. The initial goal is top-line growth. Previous McKinsey research has shown that a decline in earnings accompanied by above-average growth in revenue leads to higher total shareholder return than when companies grew more slowly and boosted their return on invested capital (Jiang & Koller 2007). But it must be underscored that spending, on its own, is no guarantee of high performance. Management must have the capacity to analyze the company's business environment so as to improve the chances that investments will be made wisely.

2. Constructing a portfolio of strategic initiatives that delivers returns exceeding the cost of capital

In the long run, top-line growth alone won't, of course, deliver shareholder value. Strategic initiatives must, at least on average, produce returns in excess of the cost of capital. A company will generally be pursuing a number of strategic initiatives at any given time. An example would be investing simultaneously in building a brand, innovating new products, and investing in new overseas markets. Not every investment in this portfolio has to earn more than its cost of capital, but ideally they should be mutually reinforcing. The goal is for the portfolio of initiatives as a whole to earn more than its aggregate cost of capital.

3. Dynamically allocating capital and talent to businesses and initiatives that create the most value

Investing for the long term does not equate to maintaining the same business mix for extended time spans. Executives must monitor the evolution of the business environment and enter or exit businesses as the competitive landscape shifts. Companies must also reallocate talent as frequently as they reallocate capital. Companies that follow these imperatives have been shown to maintain higher returns than their peers (Hall, Lovallo, & Musters 2012; Barriere, Owens, & Pobereskin 2018).

A recent example of this type of behavior is Walmart's investment in e-commerce. In order to avoid being disrupted by Amazon, in 2014 Walmart began to invest billions each year in digital commerce through acquisitions, expansion of its Silicon Valley R&D, and integration with its vast network of stores. The effort has generally been considered a success, and, as it turned out, Walmart was well positioned to benefit from the huge growth in e-commerce during the COVID-19 pandemic.

4. Generating value not only for shareholders but also for employees, customers, and other stakeholders

Companies with a long-term perspective focus on improving outcomes for all their stakeholders, not just those who own shares in the business. They have good reasons to do so. Motivated employees get more done than disgruntled ones. Well-treated suppliers work together more collaboratively. Many customers are motivated to pay extra for products that can claim lower environmental burdens.

While executives must consider trade-offs among the interests of their constituents every day, over the long term, the interests of shareholders and stakeholders converge. Most stakeholder-oriented initiatives fall into a category known as environmental, social, and governance (ESG) investments. A 2015 summary of twenty-five earlier literature reviews representing hundreds of primary studies of the impact of ESG investments on corporate financial performance found that a majority of cases (at least 63%) showed a positive impact versus only 8 percent with negative effects (and the remainder being neutral) (Friede, Busch, & Bassen 2015).

5. Staying the long-term course by resisting the temptation to take actions that boost short-term profits

The business environment is unpredictable, perhaps increasingly so. Revenue and earnings can fall for a variety of reasons, some transitory (extreme weather, ransomware, etc.), others more lasting (US–China friction, disruption by a rival, etc.). When temporary changes occur, management is likely to be tempted by maneuvers that boost short-term results to meet stock market expectations and/or the company's own guidance. Typical short-term maneuvers with long-term consequences are reducing growth-oriented investments in R&D or new resources and cutting costs in areas such as customer service that could weaken the company's competitive position. Companies with long-term perspectives resist such temptations.

A mistake that many managers make is assuming that the most vocal and active investors are representative of all investors. Roughly seven in ten shares of US companies are owned by longer-term investors: individuals, index funds, and more sophisticated long-term investors (Darr & Koller 2017). Managers can cultivate these investors by emphasizing long-term road maps over short-term guidance (Babcock & Williamson 2017). There is, in fact, no requirement for companies to provide quarterly earnings guidance, and attempting to meet the expectations of short-term investors often leads to ultimately uneconomic choices just to reduce the natural volatility in revenue and earnings.

Summary and Recommendations

The implementation of long-term oriented behaviors requires a conscious transition on the part of top managers and boards of directors. It requires adopting new behaviors and new mental models. A long-term orientation must also be communicated throughout the company and backed up by actions and reward systems.

Boards of directors currently spend too much time ensuring compliance and too little time assessing the strategies and investment plans of the businesses they direct. Directors can dive further into the strategy development process by engaging in "homework" between formal meetings, such as self-assigned industry analysis or communication with management or with long-term investors (FCLTGlobal 2019). Memos and presentations for meetings should be distributed by management well in advance. The board chair can help by ensuring that meeting agendas are short and balanced between compliance and metrics, on the one hand, and strategy and long-term planning, on the other. Adequate staff support should be available.

The board can help ensure management stays focused on the long term by confirming that strategic investments are fully funded each year and have the appropriate talent assigned to them. CEOs should be evaluated on the quality and execution of the company's strategy, the company's culture, and the strength of the management team, not just on near-term financial performance. Executive compensation should be structured over long time horizons – including time after executives have left the company.

CEOs, meanwhile, must do what they can to insulate strategic initiatives from short-term pressures, whether emanating from investors or from other business units competing for resources. The demands of short-term investors should be countered with clear, long-term strategies and outreach to longer-term investors.

Evaluations of the company's managers should strike a balance between rewards for short-term results and efforts to build long-term value. The identification and pursuit of high-risk/high-reward opportunities should be rewarded and recognized, while failures in such efforts should be analyzed but not punished. In order to make such processes easier to manage, management must identify nontraditional metrics that will make the evaluation process more transparent and that can be used to communicate more clearly to key investors and other stakeholders the progress being made toward long-term goals. Organizations such as the Sustainability Accounting Standards Board are already institutionalizing such approaches.

Naturally, not all sectors enjoy the same potential for long-term growth. Coal mining, for example, is likely a dead end – or at least a case where the interests of different stakeholder groups are irreconcilable. Nevertheless, I am confident that these management and board behaviors can benefit businesses across nearly every industry.

Given the uncertainty in the business environment, the entrepreneurial nature of strategic management, and the need for continued research on the effectiveness of long-term growth measures, the approaches laid out here and in the underlying reports that have been referenced must be viewed as preliminary. There is still a deep need for further research on topics such as board behaviors and CEO traits that are conducive to long-term performance, or executive compensation structures that give CEOs strong incentives to adopt a long-term orientation.

Even with the best research results imaginable, managing for long-term performance will remain a complex endeavor. But executives should not take this complexity as a reason to delay. The sooner they adopt long-term behaviors, the sooner they will achieve the performance gains that produce value for stakeholders over the long run.

7 Market Power and the New Antitrust: Where the Antimonopoly Narrative Goes Wrong

Gerald F. Davis

Introduction

The dawning of the third decade of the twenty-first century saw a surprising consensus across the political spectrum about the rising threat of monopoly power. Big Tech was especially suspect. On the one hand, tech platforms had become indispensable to modern life. On the other hand, Big Tech seemed to operate beyond the reach of democratic control.

The insurrection at the US Capitol on January 6, 2021, illustrates the dilemma. Tech platforms such as Facebook and Twitter provided an infrastructure for planning and executing the assault on the Capitol. Employees at both these companies sounded the alarm about the dangers lurking on their platforms – to no avail. But within forty-eight hours of the incursion, both platforms had suspended Donald Trump's account, depriving him of his preferred megaphones. Google and Apple both dropped the right-wing social media platform Parler from their app stores after it became clear that Parler had served as a key communication tool during the insurrection, and Amazon Web Services deleted its account, thus effectively removing it from the world until it found a new host.

The actions of Big Tech were quick, decisive, and effective. But they also illustrate the potential hazards of having a small number of gatekeepers with the ability to unilaterally decide who gets heard. Whatever one's political views, the fact that a president and his movement could be effectively silenced through the decisions of five business executives sits uneasily with any concept of democracy.

Although there is broad political support for reining in Big Tech, the traditional tools for regulating corporations, such as antitrust, are not well-suited to the purpose. "It's not realistic to expect antitrust to have an important influence on privacy, data security, hate speech, imminent incitements to violence, malign foreign influence, or misinformation" (Wheeler, Verveer, & Kimmelman 2020). Legal cases are slow, vigorously contested, and likely to wind up before economics-oriented judges who have lifetime appointments. Fixing the problems with Big Tech using antitrust is like doing surgery with oven mitts on.

In this section, I describe the revival of Progressive-Era antimonopolism for the digital age. In the United States, the Biden administration has gone all in on reregulating the corporation, particularly Big Tech, and antimonopolists have ascended to central positions in the Justice Department and the Federal Trade

Commission (FTC) (the two major competition authorities). But the antimonopoly narrative is tinged with nostalgia for an era that will not be coming back.
The basic building blocks for enterprise have changed due to information and
communication technologies (ICTs), and thus we need a new way to think about
corporate power (see Davis 2022 for more detail). The section closes with an
assessment of the promising and less promising approaches proffered.

The Antimonopoly Narrative

What is known as competition law everywhere else is called antitrust in the
United States. Why *anti*trust? Because the most prominent efforts to collude
with competitors to fix prices were accomplished through "trusts" that combined industry rivals under a single decision-making entity, such as Standard
Oil. The Sherman Act of 1890 was the founding document of American
antitrust, aiming to rein in the anticompetitive behavior of monopolists.

Ironically, the next fifteen years saw a massive merger movement that
combined regional companies into national corporations across dozens of
industries (Lamoreaux 1985). Many of the shortcomings of the Sherman Act
were overcome in 1914 with the creation of the FTC and the passage of the
Clayton Act, which outlawed mergers that lessened competition. The New Deal
saw the passage of the Robinson–Patman Act in 1936, which limited the ability
of vendors to offer discounts to bulk buyers such as A&P and thus protected
local retailers. Last, the Celler–Kefauver Anti-Merger Act of 1950 further
limited horizontal and vertical mergers and thus inadvertently prompted the
conglomerate merger boom of the 1960s.

For three decades after the end of World War II, the antitrust regime created
by these four laws severely limited market concentration, and corporate growth
largely took the form of diversification. Corporations such as General Electric,
Gulf & Western, Westinghouse, and ITT acquired vast portfolios that spanned
countless unrelated industries and the largest companies tended to be the most
diverse. American corporations were very big, but industries were not particularly concentrated.

This is where things stood in 1978 when Yale law professor Robert Bork
published his book *The Paradox of Antitrust*. Bork argued that the main point of
antitrust was to promote consumer welfare by keeping prices low and that the
tools of economics were indispensable for accomplishing this goal. By implication, other goals pursued under the umbrella of antitrust, such as protecting
small businesses from unfair competition, empowering labor in the face of
concentrated employment markets, or limiting the political power of corporations, were beyond the scope of antitrust.

According to latter-day antimonopolists, Bork's work had a mesmerizing effect on lawyers, judges, policymakers, and economists. Free market ideologues and their foundations funded reeducation camps for judges and "law & economics" programs in law schools that marinated legal larvae in a narrow and economic conception of antitrust. When Ronald Reagan was elected president, fellow travelers ascended to key policy positions in the Justice Department and the FTC; antitrust enforcement slipped into a four-decade coma.

The Problem with the Antimonopoly Narrative

The antimonopoly narrative has been wildly successful in changing the discourse around corporate power. It seems that, today, everyone agrees with the basic diagnosis, from Josh Hawley to Amy Klobuchar to President Joe Biden, whose July 2021 Executive Order on Promoting Competition in the American Economy proposed seventy-two initiatives to limit corporate overreach. Binyamin Appelbaum (2021) summarized the new received wisdom in August 2021, stating that "concentrations of corporate power are now the norm in the United States. A 2018 study found that concentration has increased in three-quarters of domestic industries in recent decades, giving companies greater power to raise prices, squeeze suppliers and suppress wages – and to exert outsize influence on regulators and politicians."

But the stylized facts behind the antimonopoly narrative are far more stylized than they are factual. Take the claim that 75 percent of industries have become more concentrated in the past twenty years, which is cited verbatim by Biden's executive order and in nearly every other recent antimonopoly argument. The article making this claim used Compustat data on total revenues for US-domiciled companies listed on American stock markets calculated at the three-digit NAICS industry level (Grullon, Larkin, & Michaely 2019). But the revenue figures include global sales, not just US sales, while S&P 500 companies generate 30–40 percent of their revenues overseas. Two-thirds of Netflix's subscribers are outside the United States and Canada; 67 percent of Apple's revenues are from outside the United States; most of Alphabet's revenues are from overseas.

Even if the study used only US revenues, most big corporations operate across many industries (in Apple's case, smartphones, computers, retail stores, apps, app stores, media content, and more) and throwing them all into just one industry category is seriously misleading. Anyone with passing familiarity with industrial organization economics is aware of the fatal hazards of trying to infer the state of competition on the basis of national revenue figures (Berry, Gaynor, & Scott Morton 2019). National sales figures for retail and restaurants – two industries that have genuinely become more "concentrated" at the national level – are irrelevant for the localized competition in which they engage (Hsieh & Rossi-Hansburg 2019; Rossi-Hansburg, Sarte, & Trachter 2021). And vast swaths of American industry have gone private in recent years, meaning that their revenues are absent from Compustat data.

The monopolists stand accused of raising prices and abusing their suppliers. Has Alphabet jacked up the price of Google Search, or Google Maps, or Gmail, or Chrome, or Sheets, or YouTube, or . . . anything, really? How much are you shelling out for Facebook or Instagram or WhatsApp these days? Of course, Google and Facebook's paying customers are not the "users" performing searches but the advertisers trying to sell them things. But antimonopolists rarely make the case that we should regulate these services because they are overcharging advertisers. (Privacy concerns on behalf of data "suppliers" are another matter.) Are monopolists using their power to suppress wages? The median employee at Alphabet took home $273,493 in 2020; at Facebook, it was $262,633; at Netflix, $219,577; at Microsoft, $172,142. The fortunate few that find themselves employees of tech monopolies are extravagantly compensated, in contrast to the temps, vendors, and contractors (TVCs) who make up the majority of the workforce at some of these companies.

Unfortunately for the antimonopolists, a compelling narrative sprinkled with a few anecdotes does not always work in court. As the judge who rejected the FTC's initial antitrust filing against Facebook in June 2021 put it, "It is almost as if the agency expects the court to simply nod to the conventional wisdom that Facebook is a monopolist . . . whatever it may mean to the public, 'monopoly power' is a term of art under federal law with a precise economic meaning: the power to profitably raise prices or exclude competition in a properly defined market" (Kang 2021). The simple monopoly narrative – that a high share of sales within an industry allows corporations to charge high prices and pay low wages – fits uneasily with the facts of the case for Big Tech.

What Is a Monopoly Today?

None of this is to say that Big Tech is harmless, or that corporations are benign. They are not: Corporations have helped bring about nearly every societal pathology in America today, from the opioid and obesity epidemics to the global heating that stands as an existential threat to our species. Big Tech creates distinctive hazards to democracy, privacy, and the very idea of knowledge and truth. But this is not a problem of monopoly: It is a problem of capitalism and how we understand it.

Underlying the confusion around monopoly is an ongoing shift in the organization of the economy driven by ICTs that have greatly reduced the transaction costs of using markets – of "buying," instead of "making." ICTs have changed how companies raise capital (Indiegogo), find suppliers (Alibaba), recruit labor (Uber, Mturk, Upwork), and distribute their products and services (Amazon, Shopify). In a world where any kid in a dorm room can assemble a business from online parts, the public corporation itself is an increasingly obsolete way to organize economic activity – which is why there are half as many corporations listed on the stock market today as there were twenty-five years ago (Davis 2016).

Venture capitalist Marc Andreesen famously said that "software is eating the world," and for dessert, it is dining on our map of how the economy works. A commonsense definition of monopoly is when an American industry is dominated by couple of big firms. But what if "industry" and "big" no longer work as categories for understanding the world?

What Is an Industry?

Industries are groups of firms that compete for customers in the same market or operate establishments that engage in the same kinds of activities. But many tech firms have highly ambiguous industries (and some, e.g., Coinbase, do not operate any "establishments" at all). Judged by their internal activities, most are in the "staring at a screen and typing on a keyboard" industry. Measured in terms of where they get their revenues, Google and Facebook are advertising brokers. Providing Web search or videos or social media are simply honey traps to serve up ads, which is why you are a "user" of Google, not a "customer." Similarly, Robinhood sells data to financial companies and directs order flow to others. The daytraders who use Robinhood's no-fee platform are not customers, and Robinhood is not in the brokerage industry. Meanwhile, Uber is very clear that it is not a transportation company but an online markets firm ("Prepackaged software," according to the prospectus for initial public offering).

This is not just pedantic. When the Clayton Act was passed, the corporations in the Dow Jones index made steel, copper, rubber, leather, sugar, and railroad cars – tangible products with measurable revenues and obvious competitors. But when the congressional subcommittee's majority report on tech monopolies was published in October 2020, it included reports on four "giant" conglomerates competing across many seemingly unrelated product markets: operating systems, browsers, maps, search, social networks, advertising, voice assistants, cloud computing. In many of them, users pay no cash for the product or service they receive. It is hard to imagine what the authors of the Sherman Act would have made of someone using Robinhood (a free stock-trading app) on Android (a free operating system) to trade Dogecoin (a sarcastic meme–based cryptocurrency).

What Is Big?

There are many ways to be big. Firms can be big in sales, or assets, or employment, or profit, or market capitalization. For most of the twentieth century, these all went together. Think General Motors, AT&T, or Sears. Corporations with lots of revenues tended to have lots of assets (factories, phone lines, stores) and lots of employees. They were Goliaths in all ways. Today, corporations can be giant in impact with trivially few employees or assets. When DoorDash went public in late 2020 with a mission "to grow and empower local economies," it claimed a 50 percent market share in online food delivery in the United States, with 18 million customers, 390,000 merchants, 1 million delivery people … but just 3,279 employees globally and almost nothing by way of tangible assets. (Its self-proclaimed industry is "Business services, not elsewhere classified.") Similar numbers hold across the tech sector, where tiny "disrupters" are taking down long-standing incumbents. Zoom beat Google and Microsoft and Facebook and Cisco to provide the global standard for video communication during the COVID-19 pandemic. It had 500 million downloads during 2020 and 300 million daily users by mid-2021, but employed just 4,400 workers globally and rented server space from Amazon and Oracle.

Our categories for analyzing the twentieth-century economy no longer work in the twenty-first. Yet it is clear that Big Tech corporations have become too powerful. What do we do?

Proposed Remedies

For the antimonopolists, our outdated map of the economy creates a real challenge. Antitrust may help with some very specific issues, but it is hardly the cure-all for abuses of corporate power.

What approaches have been proposed, and what are their merits? Senator Josh Hawley proposed three measures: bust up existing Big Tech companies (e.g., require Google to hive off YouTube); ban mergers and acquisitions by any company "larger than $100 billion" (by which he evidently means market cap); and expand the purview of antitrust beyond the consumer welfare standard (Hawley 2021). The first and third of these recommendations are also broadly consistent with critics at the other end of the political spectrum, such as Lina Khan, the new chair of the FTC.

If the goal is to encourage more startups and more innovation, the proposal to ban acquisitions by any company with a market cap north of $100 billion is certain to backfire. The majority – perhaps the overwhelming majority – of tech startups are created with an explicit aim to exit by being acquired (Arora, Fosfuri, & Rønde 2021). Tech founders don't want to compete with Google or Facebook – they want to get acquired by them, which assures a far more certain payday for themselves and their option-holding employees.

As for breakups, it is essential that we first recognize the diversity of business models within Big Tech. They make their money in many different ways, and there is no one-size-fits-all remedy that applies to them all. The three dominant business models are: (1) ad-funded platforms (Google Search, Facebook, Twitter); (2) transaction/matchmaking platforms that enable exchanges (Amazon, Uber, Airbnb); and (3) operating system–based ecosystem platforms (iOS, Android, Windows, AWS; see Caffarra & Scott Morton 2021). Each may require its own remedy.

Economist Paul Romer suggests a targeted approach to limit the harms of the advertising-driven business model: a graduated Pigovian tax on targeted advertisements whose rates go up for bigger companies. Much as a carbon tax would limit unwanted emissions, a targeted ad tax would limit pesky commercial intrusions on our browsing. Dave Yost (2021), Ohio's attorney general, has gone further, proposing that Google Search specifically be classified as a public utility and thus subject to the same regulations as other common carriers. Recognizing Google Search as a natural monopoly that has become essential to modern life puts it in a special category of its own to limit potential profit-driven abuses.

For transaction platforms, the biggest danger comes from gatekeepers who have exclusive or near-exclusive control over access to critical constituencies on either side of the platform (Caffarra & Scott Morton 2021). The source of a gatekeeper's power is not being "big" but being "central," standing between. It's not being the tallest building but being at the right intersection. Gatekeepers shape the ability of other firms to do business. And it is not their industry that matters so much as their business model: Do they provide access to markets or consumers not available elsewhere?

Thus, perhaps the most concerning source of corporate power in the twenty-first century is not being the biggest firm in the beer or eyeglass or auto industry, but being a gatekeeper that controls access to the building blocks of business: capital, labor, supplies, and distribution. Currently, capital markets are hard to monopolize – if it is easy to launch a stock-trading platform like Robinhood or its many competitors, it is hard to see banking as overly monopolistic. (Indeed, many entrepreneurs are launching their own currency, undermining the monopoly of the Federal Reserve.) Labor markets are also hard to monopolize, particularly with the advent of work from home: For many jobs, the potential labor market is set to become effectively global, and there is little prospect of a single labor platform (an "Uber for everything"). Supply and distribution markets, on the other hand, do have relatively dominant platforms in the form of Alibaba and Amazon. This suggests a more promising approach to antimonopoly than size (however measured) or industry concentration: target the gatekeepers that enable the creation of other businesses.

Within the American context, the most effective approach to regulating such gatekeepers is the creation of a new regulatory agency that is nimble enough to keep up with a fast-moving sector and staffed by experts who (unlike Josh Hawley) know what an application programming interface (API) is. This is the approach initially proposed by the Stigler Center in 2019 and fleshed out in greater detail by Wheeler, Verveer, and Kimmelman (2020) in their proposal for a "Digital Platform Agency," drawing on the model of the Federal Communications Commission.

Conclusion

Big Tech creates both new opportunities and new hazards for commerce and democracy. While the revived enthusiasm for Progressive-Era antitrust signals optimism for reregulating corporate power, the bigger threat is not industry concentration but the ICT-enabled reorganization of the core factor markets for enterprise. Any new regulatory efforts should start there.

8 The Emerging Technological Revolutions and Social Change

Maryann Feldman, Frederick Guy, Simona Iammarino,
and Carolin Ioramashvili

Introduction

Technology offers the potential to cure human disease, to increase productivity, and to decrease onerous and offensive jobs. But increasingly technology is embedded in a system that benefits just a few financially (Feldman, Guy, & Iammarino 2021). This section of the Element focuses on changes associated with new technologies, specifically artificial intelligence (AI) and new digital platforms, and the accompanying societal changes that are underway. The choices we make now may either increase concentrations of power or unleash the power of capitalism for the greater good.

Over the course of human history, certain technological changes have been so profound that they have fundamentally transformed society by introducing new ways of organizing work and the relationship between the factors of production. These changes are so fundamental that they affect almost every aspect of life, and we call them revolutions. The first was the Industrial Revolution (1760 to 1820), which marked the transition from craft production to a mechanized factory system, using water and steam as new sources of power, to process new materials, notably cotton; it was the cumulation of various precedents that took time to realize their potential. The development of trade and the rise of institutions conducive to business, reinforced by advances in chemistry and machine tools, changed the nature of work, with increased standards of living and increased urbanization. A second Technological Revolution (1870 to 1914) was marked by standardization and the use of interchangeable parts; it was powered by the internal combustion engine and petroleum and by electricity. New materials, including steel and alloys, communication technologies – such as the telegraph, telephone, and radio – and the advent of a transportation system based on railroads and modern shipping allowed for increased productivity, which required greater capital and new management techniques.

We are in the midst of another revolution, either the third or fourth, depending on who is counting and the criteria used. Some argue that computers were a third revolution while AI is bringing a fourth revolution. But it is difficult to tell the true situation while we are living through it. The future will reveal the reality of the relationships and their real impact. In 1987, Robert Solow famously said that the computer age was everywhere except for in the productivity statistics. This phenomenon – the Solow Paradox – was resolved when a few sectors, notably technology, retail, and wholesale, realized an acceleration of productivity growth. Still, these changes were more incremental, using new machines to automate existing processes and deliver efficiency gains. New technology firms emerged, starting with Microsoft (founded in 1975) and Apple (founded in 1976) among others, and benefited from network externalities to achieve substantial market share. These platforms are bringing about fundamental change, and the full potential of these new technologies has yet to be realized.

Technology, broadly defined as computers, cell phones, and digital technologies, allows easier access to information. They also allow for the collection of data about consumers and their behavior. New technological tools for collecting, storing, and analyzing virtually infinite amounts of information provide a new raw material that is profoundly different from physical materials. Increases in computing power, storage, and analytical tools make it possible to process, mine, and recognize patterns in data, giving machines the intelligence to interpret aspects of the world around them, to digest and learn, to make decisions, and then to take appropriate action – often without human intervention. It's this ability to learn from, and act upon, data that is so fundamental as to constitute a revolution.

More specifically, technological revolutions have always fundamentally altered the types and quality of jobs available. We are moving away from technology complementing labor to technology dictating the flow and pace of work. With increased monitoring of time and performance, humans are becoming subservient to technology.

The quality of jobs has bifurcated, with many low-skilled, low-paying jobs, while those who currently benefit due to their endowment of talent are nevertheless increasingly insecure as technology advances. This is explored in the next section.

Technological revolutions give rise to changes that are only clear in retrospect. The first Industrial Revolution was characterized by the rise of banking and insurance. The second was characterized by a wider distribution of ownership through the sale of common stocks. The trajectory of technology and technological change is dictated by the market, regulatory forces, and ownership of the means of production. Currently, there is a growing concentration of financial resources as well as an increased financialization of all aspects of our lives. This corresponds with a growth of platforms throughout the economy, which is explored in the section "Ownership of the Means of Production."

There is currently a robust debate about the modern interpretation of monopoly and the definition of infrastructure, as well as the role and responsibility of government to provide for its citizenry, and specific proposed public policy mechanisms to address inequities in the distribution of income. Certainly, solutions have had varying degrees of success in the past. Yet a new technological revolution calls for new solutions and new policies. Technologies such as blockchain or policy proposals such as universal basic income or platform cooperativism may offer more equitable solutions if allowed to flourish. This is the topic of the concluding section.

Machines in Charge: The Changing Workplace

Computers, automation, and AI affect the relationship between labor and capital in all sectors, across the entire economy. The displacement of workers by machines will likely exacerbate the gap between returns to capital and returns to labor, inducing greater substitution and a move to higher-wage jobs. A more optimistic view is that the displacement of workers by technology will, in aggregate, result in a net increase in new and more rewarding jobs. To date, the evidence is not encouraging.

Information and communication technologies have enabled a transformation of work. First, there is growth in job outsourcing and the rise of employment intermediaries that specialize in certain functions that were previously managed and coordinated within a company. Employment is no longer the clear relationship between a well-defined employer and a worker. What has been lost is the opportunity to advance within a company, with benefits and wages calibrated to the productivity of the entire company, rather than the payscale of a specific siloed occupation. Contractors have freedom to define how much they work and to set their hours, but at the same time they do not enjoy the same protections or benefits as people in traditional jobs. In the United States, contract workers do not get unemployment insurance benefits or workers' compensation if they are laid off or hurt on the job, nor are they covered by the Civil Rights Act, which prohibits discrimination based on race, sex, and other factors.

There are estimates that 20 percent of American jobs are now under contractual agreements, with an expectation that the number will increase (Noguuchim 2018). This model supplants the older model of longtime employment with one firm and generous pension and health benefits, which can be attributed to a time when workers had more bargaining power, as captured by the *Treaty of Detroit* (Levy & Temlin 2007). Technological advances coincided and reinforced the doctrine of shareholder value, which argued that firms had no responsibility other than increasing profits.

Second, new technologies allow for a monitoring of work processes that might seem to reduce workers to simple extensions of machines, performing tasks that have been difficult to automate. People now work with machines that specify tasks and monitor performance. In Amazon warehouses and various service centers, each interaction with the human being results in an email or a phone call that asks about our satisfaction, not with the system but with the human being who handled the interaction. Worried employees sometimes alert customers that their jobs and compensation are tied to these evaluations. Employees are rewarded when they perform as the algorithm requires, taking away human touch and agency.

Coders and programmers have become analogous to the factory workers of the industrial age. Certainly, they are highly educated and relatively well paid for the tasks that they perform, but new technologies allow for a disaggregation of engineering processes that have analogies with the assembly line: Few workers have control of an entire product or process, while most contribute their expertise in a highly managed and coordinated process (see, e.g., Downs 2015). Offices have replaced factories, with an array of perks designed to make it easier for workers to stay longer hours and rely on the company for their meals, entertainment, and social lives. After the COVID-19 pandemic, work is now increasingly remote as workers use their own homes as their workplace. Yet, even highly skilled workers are at risk as the technology progresses and AI learns new skills. AI allows firms to identify patterns in tactics, strategies, and weaknesses, thus changing the nature of competition, with the firms with the best technology able to dominate markets, reduce competition, and earn monopoly rents.

Even individuals who are superstars endowed with high levels of human capital and talent are at risk. Well-paid movie stars may be replaced by photorealistic automation while sports are evolving with new predictive technologies (reinforcement learning), becoming more like video games than live events. AI is able to easily recognize patterns and provide new insights that are refining both science and the arts. Serendipity, creativity, and genius become modeling elements, rather than human capabilities: AI is redefining what it means to be human. This is very different from using technology to complement human work or having machines work for people to accomplish tasks.

Pressures from capital markets and an adherence to the primacy of shareholders over other stakeholders, has led to an increased emphasis on building market share and brand, often at the expense of workers. This is reinforced by concentration in the means of production.

Ownership of the Means of Production

There has been a documented rise in monopoly power across all sectors of the economy (Berry, Gaynor, & Scott Morton 2019). One reason is increasing returns to digital technologies in which, as the number of users rises, the benefit to the consumer rises, while average costs falls and profits rise. Another reason is the retrenchment of regulation and antitrust enforcement, and the extension of intellectual property rights. Profits have been invested in building brand identity and securing market position. When competition increases innovation and consumer choice increases: Industries dominated by monopolies are less innovative and restrict consumer choice.

An important subset of network business models consists of platforms – a group of technologies used as a base upon which other applications, processes, or technologies are developed and locked down, or enclosed in a walled garden. With the rise of the platform economy, we have moved from using open networks based on universal protocols supporting email and SMS messages to messaging protocols that keep our messages within one of the various social media platforms. Competition in PC and server operating systems and standard office applications – all the elements of which are available on an open source basis – has long since been dominated by Microsoft's control of the critical, but technologically trivial, APIs and document formats. Control of a focal website where people search for and review products gives Amazon a means through which it profits from the sales of thousands of vendors while it also gathers unprecedented information on consumer purchases. Platform strategies are used in different product niches; for instance, Airbnb and Booking. com charge a fee of 15–25 percent of the proceeds from lodging provided by independent operators around the world.

There has been a significant increase in the role of the financial sector and the influence of finance in firm governance. Enhanced shareholder rights, coupled with liquidity in financial markets due to pension reforms and the 1999 repeal of the Glass–Steagall Act, have led to an increase in private equity and leveraged takeovers. This regime of financialization often appears disconnected from activity in the real economy. Billion-dollar valuations for firms with no sales or proven market have become commonplace, while other small and medium-size firms are deemed unworthy by the credit rating service algorithms of the large banks.

There has been a decline of publicly traded companies, from 8,000 in the mid-1990s to 3,600 in 2016. Three index fund managers – BlackRock, State Street Global Advisors, and the Vanguard Group – collectively hold about 25 percent of the shares in all S&P 500 companies. The stewardship decisions made by these firms have had a major impact on the governance and performance of public companies and the economy.

What Kind of World Do We Want Anyway?

The current Technological Revolution followed a developmental pathway similar to that of prior revolutions. Computers began with an uncoordinated mix of entrepreneurs, academic research projects, and hobby enthusiasts, who defined a series of open source protocols that governed the way computers communicate with one another and the flow of the internet's raw data, as well as mechanisms for sending email messages and defining the addresses of web pages. Achieving critical mass in the 1990s, these companies had seemingly unlimited sources of investment from venture capital as long as they could define a profitable business model. Based on the open technology base, a layer of for-profit companies emerged. Apple, Google, Facebook, and Amazon, among others, have become the most valuable corporations in the history of capitalism. Their business models involve tracking and influencing, and being influenced by, the activities of their customers.

Every Technology Revolution has an epicenter, and currently this is Silicon Valley. Combining market position with powerful Marshallian externalities is a powerful force that makes it difficult for less dynamic places to find niches that would bring prosperity (Feldman, Guy, & Iammarino 2020). "Places of despair" is the term used to describe the downward spiral in which jobs are no longer available, and there are few opportunities (Case & Deaton 2020).

Typically, with technology change we witness waves of creative distruction as less productive industries fail and are supplanted by new more productive ones. These periodic corrections reduce costs for entrepreneurs with new ideas. Arguably, the 2008 financial crisis was an opportunity for a realignment. However, despite the imperatives of capitalism, firms that were operating in unsustainable ways were propped up and continue with their former practices, becoming even larger in size.

Increased regulation of monopolies throughout the economy coupled with antitrust enforcement can certainly alter this trajectory. Blockchain technology may also offer a way forward that can decrease reliance on banks and financial institutions while increasing transparency in supply chains. Bitcoin was the initial application but, at its heart, blockchain is a revolutionary distributed ledger that alters the concentration of economic activity. Technology offers a way for identity and creative work to remain the provenance of individuals, rather than becoming an input for large digital platforms. The result is democratic in promoting greater equality while allowing capitalist markets to flourish and achieve their potential.

Many jobs are at risk from the rapid development of AI technologies such as robot waiters, self-driving vehicles, and reporting, writing, and translation tools.

Estimates of the impact vary, but there is a consensus that the displacement will be significant and beyond the ability of government training programs and private sector initiatives to address (Marlar 2020). To avoid a social crisis due to structural mass unemployment, universal basic income (UBI) – unconditional, regular, monetary income guaranteed as a minimum payment to all citizens – has gained global attention, with many experiments underway. Results are mixed with regard to work effort but consistently demonstrate an increase in subjective well-being, which is perhaps the point of UBI when jobs are scarce, and contractual. UBI has the potential to contribute to a healthier and more resilient society, in which individuals have the freedom to pursue activities such as art and music that have traditionally paid lower wages. Social movements such as Occupy and Lie Flat reflect growing disenchantment with the current system.

Futurists sometimes present the future as predetermined and fixed, as if the course of history is not humanly constructed. The paradox of our time is that we live with powerful technology accompanied by stagnating wages and a general social malaise. While some choose to debate issues of measurement and magnitude, it is harder to ignore the preponderance of evidence that not all individuals and communities have shared equally in economic prosperity over the past forty years since computers were introduced. A small percentage of individuals is doing well, while the incomes of the majority of the population have stagnated or declined in real terms.

It is ironic that the first two industrial revolutions brought citizens out of poverty. The current Industrial Revolution is resulting in a deskilling and degradation of work, while there seem to be no mechanisms currently to further redistribute wealth or even provide a high quality of life. Indeed, whereas the first two industrial revolutions centralized work into towns and then cities, there is every reason to believe that work will now increasingly be done at home in a return to a contractor-oriented cottage industry model. Yet, this future is not preordained; redefining the balance between labor and capital might enable technology to catapult society to a higher level with greater, shared prosperity and outcomes in keeping with a sustainable future.

9 How and Why Globalization Is Disaggregating:
The Impact of China

Orville Schell

Globalization in Retreat

For more than ten years after the turn of the century, I went to the World Economic Forum (WEF) when its discussion topics were all too often concerned with the halcyon promise of globalization. There was hardly a dark cloud in the global sky in those days. The WEF world was one filled with the ineluctable dynamic of globalization, considered a public good for all comers.

Today, the process of globalization seems to have passed an important inflection point. The whole global order, particularly the global economic and trade order, is undergoing a huge transformation. In many ways, this transformation is being driven by the very unexpected rise of authoritarianism around the world, which complicates the prospect of sourcing products at the lowest cost while paying little regard to the political system of the country. Thirty years ago, Francis Fukuyama (1992) famously proclaimed his overly optimistic view of "the end of history," and now we've sort of come to the end of the end of history. We find ourselves on the downside of an unforeseen cycle where liberal democracies, which were once perceived to be surfing on a wave of inevitable triumph, are now being challenged by various forms of latter-day authoritarianism. It's happening in Turkey, Poland, Hungary, the Philippines, and particularly in Russia with Vladimir Putin and in China with Xi Jinping.

The major catalyst of this inflection point is China, because it is pioneering a refeudalization of the global economy, even as it touts itself – as Xi Jinping did in Davos in 2019 – as a global trader. But if you look at what China has done with the internet, for instance, it's a metaphor for the kind of sequestering and resovereignization of the economy that's characteristic of the Chinese Communist Party's (CCP's) approach in many other realms of life. Xi Jinping is basically saying, "There's no such thing as a world wide web or internet for us. We want an intranet, a world unto itself, guarded against outside intrusion by gateways into China that are packet-sniffed and controlled." In other words, the intranet of the CCP is a sovereign space the enforcement of which is an aspect of a much larger idea, namely, that no interference is permissible in the internal affairs of another country. Of course, such a state is impossible in a truly globalized world.

Russia also poses a serious challenge to the global order, although it's a very different kind of problem. Whereas China is establishing itself as both a direct economic and political rival to other global powers, an economically weaker Russia is limited to asserting itself by military intervention and sowing cyber and other kinds of chaos. Over the past decade, Russia has made a series of aggressive moves: extending claims of sovereignty into Ukraine and the Arctic Ocean, countering the Western alliance in Syria, and interfering in elections in the United States and the UK. But unlike China, Russia – because its primary exports are fossil fuels and natural commodities that can potentially be substituted in a crisis – is not deeply enmeshed in the global economy. China, however, has become the world's factory, and a serious break in all its global supply chains would lead to widescale shortages of finished goods around the globe.

Global China: Separate but Enmeshed

China's vision that countries should be free to act as they please within their own sphere undermines the fundamental notion of globalization as a basis for the increase, not just of trade in goods, services, and investments, but in the exchange of people, ideas, and cultures. As globalization approached a peak before the COVID-19 pandemic that it may not reach again during the coming generation, China took full advantage of the opportunities afforded by these open exchanges. Access to the intellectual resources offered by overseas universities and companies, to foreign flows of foreign direct investment, and even to exchanges between global civil society organizations and foundations arguably sped China on its way to catching up technologically and economically with the rest of the world.

In 2019, more than a million Chinese students were studying at foreign colleges and universities, including 369,548 in the United States, by far their largest destination.[11] Chinese nationals loom particularly large among foreign students in science and engineering (S&E) programs. Over the course of the 2010s, the share of S&E doctorates awarded to citizens of China (including Hong Kong) by US universities increased from 9.9 percent to 13.4 percent (see Table 9.1). This was more than the combined total of the next two largest contributors, India and South Korea.

The United States benefited from these exchanges because the students conducted valuable research, and many have remained to become immensely valuable members of the most vibrant sectors of American society. But I don't think we had any grand strategy in mind other than wishful thinking about the

---

[11] The second- and third-largest destinations were Australia (164,317) and the UK (120,385) (Economist Intelligence Unit 2020).

Table 9.1 Chinese students earning doctorates in science and engineering at US universities

	2010	2011	2012	2013	2014	2015	2016	2017	2018	2019
All S&E* PhDs awarded	34,997	36,331	37,846	39,031	40,630	41,175	41,240	41,290	42,158	42,980
Chinese students (inc. Hong Kong) earning S&E PhDs	3,457	3,652	3,906	4,443	4,650	4,970	5,141	5,147	5,683	5,742
as % of all S&E PhDs	9.9%	10.1%	10.3%	11.4%	11.4%	12.1%	12.5%	12.5%	13.5%	13.4%

Note: * S&E includes engineering, psychology and social sciences, mathematics and computer sciences, physical sciences and earth sciences, and life sciences.

Source: Calculated from data in supplementary tables 11 and 26 in "2019 doctorate recipients from U.S. Universities," National Center for Science and Engineering Statistics, December 2020, NSF 21–308. https://ncses.nsf.gov/pubs/nsf21308/downloads.

transformative effect of exposing foreign students to the United States and its culture and values.

Now, though, scholarly exchanges between the United States and China are giving way to fear of (and to evidence of) intellectual property theft by Chinese scholars or of Americans being enticed with Chinese offers of financial support. As China moves ever more irrevocably into the role not just of competitor, but adversary, and even potential enemy, universities are increasingly being forced to decide how open they can afford to be to Chinese students, academic exchanges, and partner institutions.

China: The Moral Dimension

The deeper question is: Given the new realities of Xi Jinping's China and his belligerent "wolf warrior diplomacy" (Dai & Luqiu 2021) how open should we be to the country China is becoming? Under Xi, China is rewriting history, perfecting a surveillance state, suppressing ethnic minorities, censoring the press, jailing dissidents, grabbing territory from its neighbors, and even seeking to silence critics overseas. If we start from the standpoint of principles and conscience, rather than finance and trade, China poses an even bigger challenge to the prevailing global moral order than to supply chains.

Moral questions have a long and distinguished history in economics. Adam Smith is most famous for showing that the self-interest of each person can end up contributing to the benefit of all. But before *Wealth of Nations* (Smith 1776), he wrote *The Theory of Moral Sentiments* (Smith 1759 [1853]), an important work that made it clear that economic activity should be held up to some sort of moral standard that transcended simple profit and loss. In a passage in *The Theory of Moral Sentiments*, Smith used a hypothetical cataclysm in China to make the point that people have a propensity to ignore suffering that does not concern them directly. And yet, he continued, people often "sacrifice their own interests to the greater interests of others" (Smith 1759 [1853]: 336). He attributed this not to "benevolence" but, rather, to "reason, principle, con-science, the inhabitant of the breast, the man within, the great judge and arbiter of our conduct" (Smith 1759 [1853]: 336).

But the Chinese model, which some have proposed as an alternative to the chaotic, sometimes dysfunctional liberal democratic model,[12] is fundamentally without moral sentiment – and without all the niceties of the liberal democratic rule of law to protect the rights of the individual from the state, or from the majority. As China exports its version of global governance through outbound

---

[12] One proponent is the prime minister of Hungary, Viktor Orban; see Cabinet Office of the Prime Minister (2017).

investment – particularly via its "Belt and Road" Initiative[13] – and as these two different moral universes collide in the globalized world, the stage is indeed set for a kind of "clash of civilizations." The trade war initiated under the Trump administration (and being more or less maintained under Biden) is only the first skirmish in what could be a long and multifaceted struggle between two very different fields of political gravity.

The Great Divergence

What lies behind the train wreck with China that we now find ourselves confronting? Without going too deeply into the often-sordid history of the world's involvement in China, one can trace the pathway to the current morass through a rather amazing conceit of the West that lasted almost four decades. What came to be known as "engagement" was a policy launched in 1972, when, seeking to increase pressure on the Soviet Union, US President Richard Nixon and National Security Advisor Henry Kissinger went to China with the aim of uniting with it. But after the Soviet Union collapsed, this idea of collaborating with China lost its logic and its "operating system." In spite of the obvious warning in 1989, with the Beijing Massacre of pro-democracy demonstrators, President George H.W. Bush adopted a policy that presupposed that open markets lead to more open societies. That was the essence of "engagement": If you just keep trading and interacting, then slowly, in a kind of inevitable Hegelian way, the Leninist metal of Chinese communism will bend. This policy also ended up being pursued further by the Clinton administration, albeit after some bluster about being unwilling to "coddle tyrants from Baghdad to Beijing."[14]

There was a commonly accepted notion that history was somehow going in one direction and that, because we had divined its pulse, sooner or later China would have to change. Maybe not into becoming like us exactly, but at least becoming more convergent. It was this belief in the principle of convergence that lay at the heart of our willingness to continue to collaborate, and to support China's integration into the global market system. Our "engagement" inter-mixed with their "reform" would create a transformational sauce. Corporations, with an eye on China's large potential (at that time) market, were only too happy to follow suit and buy into the hope. And soon foreign investment was pouring into China at the expense of other industrializing economies, which saw their

---

[13] The Belt and Road Initiative is a global infrastructure development strategy adopted by the Chinese government in 2013 to invest in more than fifty countries. "Belt" refers to proposed overland routes for road and rail transportation through landlocked Central Asia. "Road" refers to sea routes through Southeast Asia to South Asia, the Middle East, and Africa.

[14] From Bill Clinton's speech at the 1992 Democratic National Convention.

growth plans stall. Another outcome was that China joined the World Trade Organization (WTO) in 2001, capping fifteen years of negotiations.

There was reason for continued optimism in the 2000s with China's president Hu Jintao. His low-key style and technocratic approach to governance were soothing to the global financial and political community, even as he oversaw crackdowns on dissent. But abroad, China was all about direct investment and the development of soft power.

We got to where we are now because when Xi Jinping came to power in 2012, he proved to be a leader of a very different kind. He wanted to see China restored to greatness. President Hu had made China wealthy, but President Xi wanted to make it powerful and respected – even feared. The West's disarray in its response to the global financial crisis in 2008 (by which time Xi had become vice president) led many in China's leadership to believe that Western democracies were so weakened and in decline that it was the optimal time to launch more assertive and aggressive policies. The goal was no longer "peaceful rise" (the official policy under Hu), implying the integration of China into the existing system outside its once-autarkic borders. The new goal was to change that system – to make the world system safe for Chinese authoritarianism, not democracy. The world did not have to become authoritarian; it just had to be accepting, compliant – even subservient.

Over the past decade, trading relations with China have become increasingly more mercantilist, as it seeks maximum leverage from the outward investment of state-owned firms for the export of Chinese goods (Aizenman, Jinjarak, & Zheng 2018). It has also used trade barriers, market access limits, and even intellectual property appropriation or theft to support the development of its high-tech sector (Atkinson 2018). China under Xi has essentially weaponized trade to make it a tool not of shareholder value but of the advancement of Party and state power in the world.

Meanwhile, China is also militarily extending its reach, starting with its brazen building and militarization of man-made islands in the South China Sea to undermine rival claims by neighboring states, such as Vietnam and the Philippines, for 12-mile territorial waters and 200-mile Exclusive Economic Zones (Patalano 2018). For example, in 2013, China refused to recognize the decision of a UN Special Arbitral Tribunal that ruled against it in the South China Sea. It was this new propensity in China to ignore international law and fundamental principles of reciprocity that highlighted the fact that we have two incompatible systems of politics and values that are irreconcilable. The disputes in need of resolution are no longer just questions of trade, balance of payments, currency exchange, and so forth. As China become more authoritarian, we have entered a world where it goes about trade, diplomatic relations, and other affairs in an increasingly different and illiberal way from the world's democracies.

This is a real problem that lands us in the middle of an unresolvable contradiction. We find that the effects of this contradiction are redounding throughout all of our once rather recklessly optimistic forms of interaction. People, nongovernmental organizations (NGOs), universities, and companies are having to scramble to one side or the other. In this new world, the global compact is beginning to break apart. Oil and water are beginning to separate. We are experiencing "decoupling" in increasingly expanding areas of life, and the COVID-19 pandemic has only exaggerated this already ineluctable process.

Beijing, for example, has deeply alienated Canada over the arrest of Huawei executive Meng Wanshou by the retaliatory kidnapping of two Canadian citizens working in China. India, after the flare-up of its border conflict with China in Ladakh, has also undergone a startling about-face in terms of its understanding of Beijing's intentions. Australia, likewise, has developed strong resistance, even antipathy, to many of China's policies after China responded to Canberra's call for a more thorough investigation into the origins of the corona-virus with punishing tariffs on Australian exports.

The international community is starting to push back. Five Australian naval ships began patrolling with the US Seventh Fleet in the South China Sea, and Delhi's commitment to the Quad alliance has become far stronger.[15] The British aircraft carrier *Queen Elizabeth* – having finished its sea trials – is steaming out to the South China Sea to engage in Freedom of Navigation Operations with the United States. Even Sweden, the archetypical neutral nation, has been galvanized into a state of real antagonism by what has shaped up to be almost an abusive relationship with China. And this dynamic is being replicated elsewhere around the world between China and other countries.

In short, whether we like it or not, we are at a point where the values proposition that divides liberal democracies from the authoritarian sphere of influence in China is coming into play more and more. These differences were given full-throated, and very base, voice under the Trump administration.[16] The Biden administration has been less noisy, but appears to be no less determined to hold the line against China's increasingly predatory efforts to project its power around the globe. And this struggle is going to fray every aspect of the global market system, from the idea of global multinationals being able to operate

---

[15] The Quadrilateral Security Dialogue is an informal strategic alliance among the United States, Japan, Australia, and India widely viewed as a response to increased Chinese economic and military power. It was initiated in 2007 and encompasses joint military exercises.

[16] See, e.g., Secretary of State Mike Pompeo's speech at the Nixon Library in July 2020 – a fulsome cry about the free world versus this other world represented by China (Pompeo 2020).

freely in any country in the world, to Chinese companies being able to launch an initial public offering on an American stock exchange or the boards of companies in China being truly international.

Looking Ahead

We seem to be heading into a period of greater and greater decoupling. Whether we like it or not, the process has begun. I do not think the decoupling will end up being complete, as it should not be – and probably cannot be – total. And I believe there are areas of mutual interest, such as climate change, public health, and disaster relief, where cooperation may still be possible. But the winds that are blowing are decidedly ill, at least as far as the old global agenda is concerned. It is unclear whether many of the twentieth-century institutions that once built and maintained that agenda – such as the WTO, the UN, international NGOs, globalized universities – will be able to adapt and survive whatever comes next (see, e.g., Akman et al. 2020).

Total decoupling is unrealistic because companies from the rest of the world have become deeply embedded with China, either through direct investment or through supplier networks. Multinationals practically sleepwalked into a situation in which they hollowed out their domestic supply bases in favor of rebuilding them in a China that was only too happy to subsidize them in exchange for access to technology, so as to soak up its huge pool of excess labor, and now it is very hard to unbake the cake. Moreover, many companies that have become reliant on selling their goods in China, such as Apple and Tesla in the United States and German automobile companies, are loath to leave.

This has placed CEOs in an awkward position. Some have vociferously advocated against decoupling, which pleases China. But the moral dimensions of conflict are increasingly raising their heads because of the audacity of China's suppression of Tibetans, its Uighur minority in Xinjiang, and the pro-democracy movement in Hong Kong. Western consumers are increasingly voting with their dollars for companies that demonstrate ethical and environmental principles, such as declining to source cotton from Xinjiang because of the likely use of forced labor there.

The CCP, however, does not take criticism lightly. And now that it has attained a real modicum of wealth and power, it has adopted an increasingly unrepentant retaliatory response mechanism. For example, soon after a statement by one clothing company, H&M, about Chinese disregard for human rights was widely disseminated on Chinese social media, all traces of the brand vanished from China's walled-off internet. The retribution was thorough, to the point that the leading Chinese app for ride hailing ceased to identify any of the company's 400 stores in China as a valid destination (Xiao 2021).

Meanwhile, policymakers in Washington on both sides of the bipartisan aisle are now so fed up with China's bellicosity, lack of reciprocity, and refusal to remedy some of the inequities that we find ourselves in a situation in which they are potentially willing to run the whole global train off the tracks. At the same time, there is also growing recognition in the United States of the need for radical home remedies, as evidenced by the $250 billion technology development legislation that is making its way through Congress (McKinnon 2021). After all, asking private US technology firms to compete with their state-subsidized rivals in China was clearly not working.

The old system of globalization depended on a certain trust and openness. Since the Mao years, China has opened its economy – up to a point. However, the trust deficit now growing between the two once-converging spheres bespeaks of a new divergence marked by growing evidence of protectionism of whole sectors of the Chinese market, companies forced to share intellectual property in exchange for access, and outright theft of American intellectual property that not only violates China's agreements through the WTO, but undermines the whole notion of a rules-based marketplace. What is most alarming is that China does not seem ready to actually remedy these inequities in its relations with the rest of the world because the economic health of their system depends on maintaining these unfair advantages.

So that is where we are today. Two very different political systems, economic systems with very different values, and very different interests. How do liberal democracies with rules-based market systems find a comfortable relationship with this top-down, state-directed command economy that the CCP has honed into a new and very powerful and dynamic form of techno-autocracy that actually works? China's economy has grown so large, and its diplomatic stance has become so aggressive, that it cannot be ignored.

We are left to ask: What are the core values of the liberal democratic world order, as set up after World War II, that cannot be compromised? How do we now deal with a paranoid China that sees "engagement" and "reform" as subversive tools secretly designed to bring about regime change? In such a circumstance, what is post-engagement engagement supposed to look like? Has such a notion become a fool's errand? We have absolutely no idea. Thus, we are left adrift like some infinitely complex, but extremely important, computer network system on which we have all come to depend but that no longer has an operating system to run it.

References

Agarwal, R., & Holmes, R. M. (2019). Let's not focus on income inequality. *Academy of Management Review*, 44(4): 450–460.

Aizenman, J., Jinjarak, Y., & Zheng, H. (2018). Chinese outwards mercantilism: The art and practice of bundling. *Journal of International Money and Finance*, 86: 31–49.

Akman, M. S., Berger, A., Botti, F., et al. (2020). The need for WTO reform: Where to start in governing world trade? G20 Insights Policy Brief. www.g20-insights.org/wp-content/uploads/2020/11/T20_TF1_PB1.pdf.

Almeida, H., Fos, V., & Kronlund, M. (2016). The real effects of share repurchases. *Journal of Financial Economics*, 119(1): 168–185.

Appelbaum, B. (2021). Break up big chicken. *New York Times*, August 21. www.nytimes.com/2021/08/17/opinion/antitrust-big-tech.html.

Arora, A., Fosfuri, A., & Rønde, T. (2021). Waiting for the payday? The market for startups and the timing of entrepreneurial exit. *Management Science*, 67 (3): 1453–1467. http://doi.org/10.1287/mnsc.2020.3627

Atkinson, R. D. (2018). Testimony of Robert D. Atkinson before the Senate Committee on Foreign Relations, Subcommittee on Multilateral International Development, Multilateral Institutions, and International Economic, Energy, and Environmental Policy, Hearing on a Multilateral and Strategic Response to International Predatory Economic Practices, May 9. https://bit.ly/3vOBSFE/.

Aum, S., & Shin, Y. (2020). Why is the labor share declining? *Federal Reserve Bank of St. Louis Review*, 102(4): 413–428. https://doi.org/10.20955/r.102.413-28

Babcock, A., & Williamson, S. K. (2017). Moving beyond quarterly guidance: A relic of the past. FCLTGlobal.org. https://bit.ly/3OF7V3k/.

Badger, S. (2020). Mars launches independent economics of mutuality foundation. The old model of capitalism needs to evolve – it's time for a new roadmap. *MARS.com*, September 9. www.mars.com/news-and-stories/articles/economics-mutuality-foundation/.

Barriere, M., Owens, M., & Pobereskin, S. (2018). Linking talent to value. *McKinsey Quarterly* (June). https://mck.co/39s8uO1/.

Barton, D., & Wiseman, M. (2015). Where boards fall short. *Harvard Business Review*, 93(1–2): 98–104.

Barton, D., Manyika, J., Koller, T., et al. (2017). Measuring the economic impact of short-termism. McKinsey Global Institute Discussion Paper. https://mck.co/3KiNWUR/.

Bebchuk, L. A., & Fried, J. M. (2004). *Pay without Performance: The Unfulfilled Promise of Executive Compensation*. Cambridge, MA: Harvard University Press.

Bebchuk, L. A., Fried, J. M., & Walker, D. I. (2002). Managerial power and rent extraction in the design of executive compensation. *University of Chicago Law Review*, 69(3): 751–846.

Berry, S., Gaynor, M., & Scott Morton, F. (2019). Do increasing markups matter? Lessons from empirical industrial organization. *Journal of Economic Perspectives*, 33(3): 44–68. http://doi.org/10.1257/jep.33.3.44

Bodolica, V., & Spraggon, M. (2009). Merger and acquisition transactions and executive compensation: A review of the empirical evidence. *Academy of Management Annals*, 3(1): 109–181.

Borisova, G., Salas, J. M., & Zagorchev, A. (2019). CEO compensation and government ownership. *Corporate Governance: An International Review*, 27 (2): 120–143.

Bork, R. H. (1978). *The Antitrust Paradox: A Policy at War with Itself*. New York: Basic.

Brauer, M. F. (2013). The effects of short-term and long-term oriented managerial behavior on medium-term financial performance: Longitudinal evidence from Europe. *Journal of Business Economics and Management*, 14(2): 386–402.

Business Roundtable (2019). Business Roundtable redefines the purpose of a corporation to promote "an economy that serves all Americans."August 19. www.businessroundtable.org/business-roundtable-redefines-the-purpose-of-a-corporation-to-promote-an-economy-that-serves-all-americans/.

Cabinet Office of the Prime Minister (2017). The old globalisation model is obsolete, May 16. https://miniszterelnok.hu/the-old-globalisation-model-is-obsolete/.

Caffarra, C., & Scott Morton, F. (2021). The European Commission Digital Markets Act: A Translation.

Case, A., & Deaton, A. (2020). *Deaths of Despair and the Future of Capitalism*. Princeton, NJ: Princeton University Press.

Cheng, Y., Harford, J., & Zhang, T. (2015). Bonus-driven repurchases. *Journal of Financial and Quantitative Analysis*, 50(3): 447–475.

Conyon, M. J., & Peck, S. I. (1998). Board control, remuneration committees, and top management compensation. *Academy of Management Journal*, 41 (2): 146–157.

Costco. (2021). Corporate Profile. https://investor.costco.com/corporate-profile-2/.

Cyert, R. M., & March, J. G. (1963). *A Behavioral Theory of the Firm*. Englewood Cliffs, NJ: Prentice-Hall.

Dai, Y., & Luqiu, L. R. (2021). China's "wolf warrior" diplomats like to talk tough. *Washington Post*, May 12. www.washingtonpost.com/politics/2021/05/12/chinas-wolf-warrior-diplomats-like-talk-tough/.

Darr, R., & Koller, T. (2017). How to build an alliance against corporate short-termism. *McKinsey.com*, January 30. https://tinyurl.com/4uh4zvx8/.

Davis, G. F. (2016). *The Vanishing American Corporation: Navigating the Hazards of a New Economy*. Oakland, CA: Berrett-Koehler.

Davis, G. F. (2022). *Taming Corporate Power in the Twenty-First Century*. Cambridge: Cambridge University Press.

de Vaan, M., Elbers, B., & DiPrete, T. A. (2019). Obscured transparency? Compensation benchmarking and the biasing of executive pay. *Management Science*, 65(9): 4299–4317.

Downs, P. (2015). Coders are becoming the industrial workers of the 21st century. Will they organize? *In These Times*, March 19.

Economist Intelligence Unit (2020). How will the coronavirus affect outbound Chinese students? September 25. www.eiu.com/n/how-will-the-coronavirus-affect-outbound-chinese-students/.

Edmans, A., Gabaix, X., & Jenter, D. (2017). Executive compensation: A survey of theory and evidence. In B. E. Hermalin & M. S. Weisbach (eds.), *Handbook of the Economics of Corporate Governance* (pp. 383–539). Amsterdam: Elsevier.

Faulkender, M., & Yang, J. (2010). Inside the black box: The role and composition of compensation peer groups. *Journal of Financial Economics*, 96(2): 257–270.

FCLTGlobal (2019). The long-term habits of a highly effective corporate board. *FCLTGlobal.com*. https://tinyurl.com/bwcxvxjt/.

Feldman, M., Guy, F., & Iammarino, S. (2020). Gathering around big tech: How the market for acquisitions reinforces regional inequalities in the US. Kenan Institute of Private Enterprise Research, Paper No. 21–01.

Feldman, M., Guy, F., & Iammarino, S. (2021). Regional income disparities, monopoly and finance. *Cambridge Journal of Regions, Economy and Society*, 14(1): 25–49.

Fich, E. M., Starks, L. T., & Yore, A. S. (2014). CEO deal-making activities and compensation. *Journal of Financial Economics*, 114(3): 471–492.

Fink, L. (2021) Letter to CEOs. www.blackrock.com/us/individual/2021-larry-fink-ceo-letter/.

Flammer, C., & Bansal, P. (2017). Does a long-term orientation create value? Evidence from a regression discontinuity. *Strategic Management Journal*, 38 (9): 1827–1847.

Flammer, C., Hong, B., & Minor, D. (2019). Corporate governance and the rise of integrating corporate social responsibility criteria in executive compensation: Effectiveness and implications for firm outcomes. *Strategic Management Journal*, 40(7): 1097–1122.

Frey, B. S., & Osterloh, M. (2005). Yes, managers should be paid like bureaucrats. *Journal of Management Inquiry*, 14(1): 96–111.

Friede, G., Busch, T., & Bassen, A. (2015). ESG and financial performance: Aggregated evidence from more than 2000 empirical studies. *Journal of Sustainable Finance & Investment*, 5(4): 210–233.

Fukuyama, F. (1992). *The End of History and the Last Man*. New York: Free Press.

George, B. (2003). *Authentic Leadership: Rediscovering the Secrets to Creating Lasting Value*. San Francisco, CA: Jossey-Bass.

Goldin, I., Koutroumpis, P., Lafond, F., & Winkler, J. (2021). Re-evaluating the sources of the recent productivity slowdown. Vox EU and Center for Economic and Policy Research. https://voxeu.org/article/re-evaluating-sources-recent-productivity-slowdown/.

Graham, J. R., Harvey, C. R., & Rajgopal, S. (2005). The economic implications of corporate financial reporting. *Journal of Accounting and Economics*, 40 (1–3): 3–73.

Greer, T. Xi Jinping in translation: China's guiding ideology. *Palladium*, May 31. https://palladiummag.com/2019/05/31/xi-jinping-in-translation-chinas-guiding-ideology/.

Grinstein, Y., & Hribar, P. (2004). CEO compensation and incentives: Evidence from M&A bonuses. *Journal of Financial Economics*, 73(1): 119–143.

Grullon, G., Larkin, Y., & Michaely, R. (2019). Are US industries becoming more concentrated? *Review of Finance*, 23(4): 697–743. https://doi.org/10.1093/rof/rfz007

Haack, P., & Sieweke, J. (2018). The legitimacy of inequality: Integrating the perspectives of system justification and social judgment. *Journal of Management Studies*, 55(3): 486–516.

Hall, S., Lovallo, D., & Musters, R. (2012). How to put your money where your strategy is. *McKinsey Quarterly*, March. https://tinyurl.com/3zww979x/.

Hawley, J. (2021). The big tech oligarchy calls out for trustbusters. *Wall Street Journal*, April 30. www.wsj.com/articles/the-big-tech-oligarchy-calls-out-for-trustbusters-11619816008/.

Hayes, S. C., Hayes, L. J., & Reese, H. W. (1988). Finding the philosophical core: A review of Stephen C. Pepper's *World Hypotheses: A Study in Evidence*. *Journal of the Experimental Analysis of Behavior*, 50: 97–111.

Hoffmann, C., Wulf, T., & Stubner, S. (2016). Understanding the performance consequences of family involvement in the top management team: The role of long-term orientation. *International Small Business Journal*, 34(3): 345–368.

Hsieh, C.-T., & Rossi-Hansberg, E. (2019). The industrial revolution in services. National Bureau of Economic Research, Working Paper 25968. www.nber.org/papers/w25968/.

Hunt, V., Simpson, B., & Yamada, Y. (2020). The case for stakeholder capitalism. McKinsey & Company. www.mckinsey.com/business-functions/strategy-and-corporate-finance/our- insights/the-case-for-stakeholder-capitalism, 2.

Jelinek, C. (2021). Testimony of Craig Jelinek, President and CEO of Costco Wholesale Corporation Before the U.S. Senate Committee on the Budget, February 25. www.budget.senate.gov/download/craig-jelinek-testimony/.

Jiang, B., & Koller, T. (2007). How to choose between growth and ROIC. *McKinsey Quarterly*. https://tinyurl.com/da5kv4mn/.

Joly, H. (2021). Leadership principles for the next era of capitalism. www.hubertjoly.org/leadership-principles-for-the-next-era-of-capitalism/.

Joly, H., & Lambert, C. (2021). *The Heart of Business: Leadership Principles for the Next Era of Capitalism*. Boston, MA: Harvard Business Review Press.

Kang, C. (2021). Judge throws out 2 antitrust cases against Facebook. *New York Times*, June 28. www.nytimes.com/2021/06/28/technology/facebook-ftc-lawsuit.html.

Kim, E. H., Maug, E., & Schneider, C. (2018). Labor representation in governance as an insurance mechanism. *Review of Finance*, 22(4): 1251–1289.

Lamoreaux, N. R. (1985). *The Great Merger Movement in American Business, 1895–1904*. Cambridge: Cambridge University Press.

Lattanzio, G., Megginson, W. L., & Sanati, A. (2021). Dissecting the listing gap: Mergers, private equity, or regulation? http://dx.doi.org/10.2139/ssrn.3329555

Lazonick, W. H. (2014). Profits without prosperity. *Harvard Business Review*, 92(9): 46–55.

Lazonick, W. H. (2015). Stock buybacks: From retain-and-reinvest to down-size-and-distribute. www.brookings.edu/wp-content/uploads/2016/06/lazonick.pdf.

Lazonick, W. (2019). The theory of innovative enterprise: Foundations of economic analysis. In T. Clarke, J. O'Brien, & C. R. T. O'Kelley (eds.), *The Oxford Handbook of the Corporation* (pp. 490–514). Oxford: Oxford University Press.

Lazonick, W., & Shin, J. S. (2020). *Predatory Value Extraction: How the Looting of the Business Corporation Became the US Norm and How Sustainable Prosperity Can Be Restored*. Oxford: Oxford University Press.

Levy, F., & Temlin, P. (2007). Inequality and institutions in 20th century America. National Bureau of Economic Research, Working Paper 13106. www.nber.org/papers/w13106/.

March, J. G., & Olsen, J. P. (2011). The logic of appropriateness. In R. E. Goodin (ed.), *The Oxford Handbook of Political Science* (pp. 478–497). Oxford: Oxford University Press.

Marlar, J. (2020). Assessing the impact of new technologies on the labor market. Report to the US Department of Labor, Bureau of Labor Statistics.

Marshall, R. (2017). Out of whack: US CEO pay and long-term investment returns. MSCI ESG Research. https://tinyurl.com/3jk6dwmd/.

Mayer, C., Strine, L., & Winter, J. (2020). Fifty years later, Milton Friedman's shareholder value doctrine is dead. *Fortune Magazine*, September 13.

McKinnon, J. D. (2021). Senate approves $250 billion bill to boost tech research. *Wall Street Journal*, June 8. www.wsj.com/articles/senate-approves-250-billion-bill-to-boost-tech-research-11623192584/.

Mishel, L., & Wolfe, J. (2019). CEO compensation has grown 940% since 1978. Economic Policy Institute, Washington, DC. https://files.epi.org/pdf/171191.pdf.

Murphy, K. J., & Sandino, T. (2019). Compensation consultants and the level, composition and complexity of CEO pay. *Accounting Review*, 95(1): 311–341.

Noguuchim, Y. (2018). Freelanced: The rise of the contract workforce. National Public Radio/ Marist Poll, January 22. www.npr.org/2018/01/22/578825135/rise-of-the-contract-workers-work-is-different-now/.

Patalano, A. (2018). When strategy is "hybrid" and not "grey": Reviewing Chinese military and constabulary coercion at sea. *Pacific Review*, 31(6): 811–839.

Patel, N. 2020. The Motley Fool. www.fool.com/investing/2020/11/08/if-you-invested1000-in-costcos-ipo-this-is-how-mu/.

Piketty, T. (2014). *Capital in the Twenty-First Century*. Cambridge: Harvard University Press.

Pompeo, M. R. (2020). Communist China and the free world's future. Richard Nixon Presidential Library, July 23. https://2017-2021.state.gov/communist-china-and-the-free-worlds-future-2/index.html.

Prasad, A. (2018). When is economic inequality justified? *Business Horizons*, 61(6): 855–862.

Rossi-Hansberg, E., Sarte, P.-D., & Trachter, N. (2021). Diverging trends in national and local concentration. *NBER Macroeconomics Annual*, 35: 115–150. https://doi.org/10.1086/712317

Schiff, M., & Lewin, A. Y. (1968). Where traditional budgeting fails. *Financial Executive*, 36(5): 50–62.

Schiff, M., & Lewin, A. Y. (1970). The impact of people on budgets. *Accounting Review*, 45(2): 259–268.

Schiff, M., & Lewin, A. Y. (1974). *Behavioral Aspects of Accounting*. Englewood Cliffs, NJ: Prentice Hall.

Sisodia, R. (2018). The role of boards in the age of conscious capitalism. https://youtu.be/NypVrkWzrLU/.

Sisodia, R., Sheth, J., & Wolfe, D. (2014). *Firms of Endearment: How World Class Companies Profit from Passion and Purpose*, 2nd ed. Upper Saddle River, NJ: Pearson Education.

Smith, A. (1759) [1853]. *The Theory of Moral Sentiments*, 6th ed. London: Strahan & Cadell.

Smith, A. (1776). *An Inquiry into the Nature and Causes of the Wealth of Nations*. London: Strahan & Cadell.

Smith, A. (1976a) [1776]. *An Inquiry into the Nature and Causes of the Wealth of Nations*. 2 vols. Edited by R. H. Campbell & A. S. Skinner. Oxford: Oxford University Press.

Smith, A. (1976b) [1759]. *The Theory of Moral Sentiments*. Edited by D. D. Raphael & A. L. Macfie, Oxford: Oxford University Press.

Smith, A. (1980a) [1795]. *Essays on Philosophical Subjects*. Edited by W. P. D. Wightman. Oxford: Oxford University Press.

Smith, A. (1980b). *Lectures on Jurisprudence*. Edited by R. L. Meek, D. D. Raphael, & P. G. Stein. Oxford: Oxford University Press.

Sneader, K., Williamson, S. K., Koller, T., Potter, V., & Babcock, A. (2021) Corporate long-term behaviors: How CEOs and boards drive sustained value creation. McKinsey & Company and FCLTGlobal.https://tinyurl.com/9n98njbw/.

Steele, R., & Albright, C. (2004). Games managers play at budget time. *MIT Sloan Management Review*, 45(3): 81–84.

Stigler Committee on Digital Platforms (2019). Stigler Committee on Digital Platforms: Final report. Stigler Center for the Study of the Economy and the State. www.chicagobooth.edu//media/research/stigler/pdfs/digital-platforms—committee-report—stigler-center.pdf.

Stout, L. (2012). *The Shareholder Myth: How Putting Shareholders First Harms Investors, Corporations and the Public*. San Francisco, CA: Berrett-Koehler.

Subcommittee on Antitrust, Commercial and Administrative Law of the Committee on the Judiciary (2020). Investigation of competition in digital markets: Majority staff report and recommendations.

Sun, J., & Cahan, S. (2012). The economic determinants of compensation committee quality. *Managerial Finance*, 38(2): 188–205.

Tahir, M., Ibrahim, S., & Nurullah, M. (2019). Getting compensation right: The choice of performance measures in CEO bonus contracts and earnings management. *British Accounting Review*, 51(2): 148–169.

Teece, D. J. (2009). *Dynamic Capabilities and Strategic Management: Organizing for Innovation and Growth*. Oxford: Oxford University Press.

Tsui, A. S., Enderle, G., & Jiang, K. (2018). Income inequality in the United States: Reflections on the role of corporations. *Academy of Management Review*, 43(1): 156–168.

United States Census Bureau (2021). 2017 SUSB annual data tables by establishment industry. www.census.gov/data/tables/2017/econ/susb/2017-susb-annual.html.

Wang, T., & Bansal, P. (2012). Social responsibility in new ventures: Profiting from a long-term orientation. *Strategic Management Journal*, 33(10): 1135–1153.

West, D. (2011). *The Purpose of the Corporation in Business and Law School Curricula*. Washington, DC: Brookings Institution Press.

Westphal, J. D., & Zajac, E. J. (1997). Defections from the inner circle: Social exchange, reciprocity, and the diffusion of board independence in U.S. corporations. *Administrative Science Quarterly*, 42(1): 161–183.

Wheeler, T., Verveer, P., & Kimmelman, G. (2020). New digital realities; new oversight solutions in the U.S.: The case for a digital platform agency and a new approach to regulatory oversight. Harvard Kennedy School Shorenstein Center on Media, Politics and Public Policy. https://shorensteincenter.org/wp-content/uploads/2020/08/New-Digital-Realities_August-2020.pdf.

Williamson, O. E. (1963). A model of rational managerial behavior. In R. M. Cyert & J. G. March (eds.), *A Behavioral Theory of the Firm* (pp. 237–252). Englewood Cliffs, NJ: Prentice-Hall.

Williamson, S. K. (2021). A lesson in stakeholder capitalism from the failed super league. *Forbes*, April 21. www.forbes.com/sites/sarahkeohanewilliamson/2021/04/21/a-lesson-in-stakeholder-capitalism-from-the-failed-super-league/?sh=4cd56f985eaa/.

Xiao, E. (2021). H&M is erased from Chinese e-commerce over Xinjiang stance. *Wall Street Journal*, March 25. www.wsj.com/articles/h-m-is-erased-from-chinese-e-commerce-over-xinjiang-stance-11616695377/.

Yost, D. (2021). Let's make Google a public good. *New York Times,* July 7. www.nytimes.com/2021/07/07/opinion/google-utility-antitrust-technology.html.

Cambridge Elements ☰

Reinventing Capitalism

Arie Y. Lewin
Duke University

Arie Y. Lewin is Professor Emeritus of Strategy and International Business at Duke University, Fuqua School of Business. He is an Elected Fellow of the Academy of International Business and a Recipient of the Academy of Management inaugural Joanne Martin Trailblazer Award. Previously, he was Editor-in-Chief of *Management and Organization Review* (2015–2021) and the *Journal of International Business Studies* (2000–2007), founding Editor-in-Chief of *Organization Science* (1989–2007), and Convener of Organization Science Winter Conference (1990–2012). His research centers on studies of organizations' adaptation as co-evolutionary systems, the emergence of new organizational forms, and adaptive capabilities of innovating and imitating organizations. His current research focuses on de-globalization and decoupling, the Fourth Industrial Revolution, and the renewal of capitalism.

Till Talaulicar
University of Erfurt

Till Talaulicar holds the Chair of Organization and Management at the University of Erfurt where he is also the Dean of the Faculty of Economics, Law and Social Sciences. His main research expertise is in the areas of corporate governance and the responsibilities of the corporate sector in modern societies. Professor Talaulicar is Editor-in-Chief of *Corporate Governance: An International Review*, Senior Editor of *Management and Organization Review*, and serves on the Editorial Board of *Organization Science*. Moreover, he has been Founding Member and Chairperson of the Board of the International Corporate Governance Society (2014–2020).

Tsuyoshi Numagami, *Hitotsubashi University, Japan*
Margit Osterloh, *University of Basel, Switzerland*
Andreas Georg Scherer, *University of Zurich, Switzerland*
Blair Sheppard, *PwC, USA*
Jeffrey Sonnenfeld, *Yale University, USA*
John Sutton, *LSE, UK*
David Teece, *UC Berkeley, USA*
Anne S. Tsui, *University of Notre Dame, USA*
Alain Verbeke, *University of Calgary, Canada*
Henk Volberda, *University of Amsterdam, The Netherlands*
Mira Wilkins, *Florida International University, USA*
Sarah Williamson, *FCLTGlobal, USA*
Arjen van Witteloostuijn, *VU Amsterdam, The Netherlands*
George Yip, *Imperial College London, UK*

About the Series

This series seeks to feature explorations about the crisis of legitimacy facing capitalism today, including the increasing income and wealth gap, the decline of the middle class, threats to employment due to globalization and digitalization, undermined trust in institutions, discrimination against minorities, global poverty and pollution. Being grounded in a business and management perspective, the series incorporates contributions from multiple disciplines on the causes of the current crisis and potential solutions to renew capitalism.

Panmure House is the final and only remaining home of Adam Smith, Scottish philosopher and 'Father of modern economics'. Smith occupied the House between 1778 and 1790, during which time he completed the final editions of his master works: *The Theory of Moral Sentiments* and *The Wealth of Nations*. Other great luminaries and thinkers of the Scottish Enlightenment visited Smith regularly at the House across this period. Their mission is to provide a world-class twenty-first-century center for social and economic debate and research, convening in the name of Adam Smith to effect positive change and forge global, future-focussed networks.

Cambridge Elements ≡

Reinventing Capitalism

Printed in the United States
by Baker & Taylor Publisher Services